For Those Who Awaken

For Those Who Awaken

A Spiritual Story of a Bipolar Journey

By

OLIVER DAVIDIAN

Copyright © 2014 by Oliver Davidian

www.forthosewhoawaken.com

ISBN-10 : 0615954294
ISBN-13 : 978-0-615-95429-5
Library of Congress Catalog Card Number: 2014931182
For Those Who Awaken, McCloud, Ca

- Dedicated to -

God & Guru

Jesus Christ & Paramahansa Yogananda

Author's Acknowledgments

Special thanks to family friend and brother in joys and sorrows, Friar Gratian Buttarazzi, O.F.M. for encouraging me to share my story as a gift of the heart to others who also have struggled with a bipolar mind.
Victory to us All.

Oliver Davidian

January 20, 2014

CONTENTS

"To Understand Everything is to Forgive Everything"

- Buddha

Preface

MANNA OF THE HEART

*O*nce upon a time there was a knocking at The Door. Just on the Other Side, yet a world away, sat a princess. In her lap she held the story of a magical journey, a tale sculpted solely by the hands of fantasy and imagination . . .

Isn't it wonderful that in the midst of all the turmoil in our lives, at times, we are permitted to briefly escape the reality that lies all around us? Perhaps these moments of freedom are one of the greatest graces the love of God has brought us. Fantasy allows us to quietly escape the complicated web that reality weaves. It lives deep within our hearts, and it is where sleeping dreams awaken like tiny seeds as they slowly make their way through the soil until the light of day shines upon their first leaves. Within the realms of fantasy anything is possible. It is where we aspire to greatness. It is where creativity and inspiration unite to create a wonder and amazement that is all around us. It is the magic that shouts for each of us to reach our hands up to the heavens and scream with glee as we pursue our hopes and our dreams! Fantasy is the freedom we feel when a cool wind brushes the side of our faces. The breeze brushes our cheeks so smoothly and with so much love. It whispers in our ears, reminding us of the things that matter; love and peace and freedom. Fantasy is the magic of Merlin and tales of the Druids. Fantasy is love's creation. Its home is the heart.

Imagination, the door that leads to the heart, lives in a place where children run and play. It is where loved ones dance and sing. Imagination is what creates the future and calls to our hearts. How wonderful and truly poetic is it that this gift was given to us as children and somehow can be unmasked once again as adults? The dance between fantasy and imagination is a dance children seem to have mastered. They dance every day and every minute, right before our eyes, but somehow we are blind.

Unfortunately, most of us have forgotten how this dance works. You see, while we were living in the bliss of infancy, in fact, probably the day we were born, there was another voice that spoke to us. At first, and for quite a while, we didn't even hear what this voice was saying.

As time passed, slowly for some, and quickly for others, we all began hearing the sounds of reality. Reality came knocking on our door every day, and even when we did not answer, it still shouted its lessons. Sadly, these lessons were often in conflict with the harmony of imagination and fantasy. The teachings of imagination and fantasy had come so easily and naturally but these new teachings were firm and cold. Slowly but surely, the seeds of reality began to grow. Reality had begun weaving its web. And what a web! *But was it Reality?* Slowly creeping up from behind, always preaching, always hammering its lesson into our minds, "reality" is a tough teacher, calm, cool, methodical, and relentless. Everyone will hear its message and at some point, a battle takes place. Fantasy and imagination suffer many blows and sometimes they seem to fall asleep at the hands of the tormentor. Many dreams and desires have been killed in this way.

Luckily, hidden deep within our hearts, the same excitement and wonder we felt as children still live. This inner radiance often falls asleep during our battle but it cannot be killed. Love and purity still live within, and once again we will all shine like the sun! The trick is to find the heart and reopen the doors we have shut. This is a journey that involves the greatest amounts of strength and passion we have. It requires all our hearts. It requires all our souls. It requires all of who we are.

The reward to those who choose to take this journey is a type of second awakening. During this awakening, we discover wonderful treasures that love and life have brought us. It's almost as if the entire world transforms right before our eyes. Problems once as tall as the snow covered mountains disappear. Fear and worries fade. A loving energy seems to bubble up from a calm place deep inside and bursts out into the world through our laughter and smiles. Light seems to flow from our limbs and surround us. Once again life is magic, and possibilities seem endless as confidence flows.

What alchemy has taken place? What grace of God has brought these ecstatic waves of love? Perhaps what has happened is that we have been given a great gift; a gift that allows those of us who have searched heart, mind, and soul, to once again have peace. A gift that is attained by soothing the burning desire within us all, this gift of gold brings love and balance to our lives. It returns our self-esteem. It reunites and allows us to once more hear the voice of our heart within. This love inside heals our hearts during the hard times and comforts us when we are lonely. It walks with us in our journeys and carries us when we cannot go on. The most beautiful and liberating part of this gift is that imagination, fantasy, and reality live with one another, and all can be in harmony. This is God's gift of love, and it lives on forever within each of us.

Fantasy, imagination, love, and truth, are what this story is about. They are truly the stuff of which dreams are made. For those who awaken, this is a story about a journey. It took place quite a while ago, but it remains as if burned into the very fiber of my soul. If I put my mind upon it, it is as if stepping into a living memory preserved for the ages by sheer intensity. Clouded at times, yes, but not a drop has been lost or dimmed by the click of time.

The nightmare descended upon me in my 20th year like a thick layer of swirling fog, clouding my vision and even my thoughts. Within its mist emerged a storm, a storm on the ocean of my mind, demanding nothing less than a total, complete, and honest search of my entire self and the kingdom I'd built my life upon. The story I tell is my best attempt to capture the storm, and the peace that followed. To achieve this I had to produce the chaos of insanity in a lucid form. In that light, time is distorted and the line between fiction and non-fiction is blurred and crossed as imagination and creativity are woven throughout the tale. Still, I deeply feel I have framed a portrait that reflects the experience of my heart.

I now reach into my treasure chest and pull out my gift to you. From my garden, I am honored to give you a White Rose along with its sister, the Red Rose of Passion.

FOR THOSE WHO AWAKEN

"Never regret thy fall,
O Icarus of the fearless flight
For the greatest tragedy of them all
Is never to feel the burning light."

- Oscar Wilde -

One

HOW IT ALL BEGAN

*S*ome destinies are written long ago. Like gentle brushstrokes etched on sand-covered beaches by spirit-inspired winds, or even tablets carved in stone, there are moments in life which change us, sometimes forever. My moment came early. The clouds parted and life embraced me within tender arms of love while in the midst of a great storm. I shall never forget. I was only twenty.

I'm 30 now, so it's been close to ten years since the final sunset of my life as a sleeping being amidst a world of living beauty. To put it concretely, it's been ten years since I had what I consider to be a spiritual awakening. Others have called it by many other names – psychosis, mania, delusion, hallucination. It was not filled with fairies and cotton candy. It was a storm of darkness and light that very nearly killed me. Whatever force got ahold of me, it was too much bear, and in my braking, something was born, a spark was lit.

The road to the present moment has not been an easy one. During the last ten years of my life I've been deeply engaged on a spiritual quest. The fuel for the fire seems to be periods of joy and great sorrow, suffering. There have been so many fitful efforts to reconnect with the divine memory stamped and imprinted in the caverns of my heart during my awakening, so many nights with tears in my eyes, praying to the Creator of All, calling out and marching back into the darkness to find the light once again. So many books. So many meditations. So many surrenders. So many births. So many deaths. These are what brought me here. I have been searching for peace while enduring the struggles arising from a bipolar mind not fully under my control. I have chosen to seek tranquility upon the path of spirituality.

Today is my first day at the Ashram. My heart has called me here, to the present moment, deeply considering the path of a monastic. I'm writing in the comfort of a cozy little room, one of the many cabins here at Hidden Valley in Escondido, part of the Self Realization Fellowship and home to monks and a collection of residents from around the world. Most are here simply to experience and bathe in the peace of this serene way of life, while others are wondering if this might be the destination of their heart's call.

Years ago I was blessed in finding a great teacher, Paramahansa Yogananda, a mystic and yogi, a Swami who came to the West and brought with him the teachings of deep meditation and higher states of consciousness. These, he artfully and carefully blended with Christianity to form a path which has become liberating and dear to my heart and mind, the perfection of Christ, and the wisdom of direct experience through yoga. Now, I'm trying to decide if I will walk in his footsteps, as a monk and hopefully as a witness to the existence of a divine love. In these moments, my heart calls me in many directions, and I must admit, all seem utterly beautiful.

What thoughts and experiences combine to motivate a person to renounce the world and seek God in the silence of a monastery? Perhaps they are quite similar to my own. Perhaps the fibers of their cloaks are made of the same joys and sorrows that you will find in this book. Perhaps the quiet setting of an ashram will provide the perfect soil from which my leaves may sprout and grow onward to the heavens? At the same time, my heart often calls to share the waters of peace and compassion that I now feel. Perhaps I have something to share with others that can only be done in the midst of the world. Perhaps the flood of emotions I feel are the very same waters we all feel and long for. I wonder what will I choose? What path will I take? Whatever path the waters blaze, wherever my heart leads, I hope to follow with no resistance, and I hope I am able to share every drop that rains down upon me. As I've learned, surrender brings peace.

So now let me take you back to the beginning. Let me take you to where it all began, the dark night and awakening of my soul ten years ago. Come with me once again and together, let us live the dream. A poet would say it began ages ago, in a different time, in a different place, in a different life, but I tell you it was like yesterday, at least for me, a ten-year-old yesterday that exists somewhere in the ether, frozen out of time.

The birth of my transformation, the spark that lit the fires of my search for a deeper truth and joy within myself, truly can only be said to have begun some time during my fraternity's initiation. I had turned twenty a few months earlier in October and I was attending San Diego State University. The second semester of my junior year of college was about to begin and I had returned to school after the Christmas break.

The initiation consisted of one "hell week" of living at the frat house with all the other pledges, followed by a three day formal indoctrination. It was not a watered down ceremony merely to stand as a symbol and rite of passage into the inner circle of brotherhood. This was nothing less than a powerful tool carefully designed to open the mind and heart, to look within and see what dwells there.

While I consider the ritual sacred and beautiful to this day, it was not conducted by an experienced ritualist or someone with any understanding of psychology, the power of the mind, or the potential dangers it could wreak upon a vulnerable young man. I was not initiated by some spiritual master, but by a bunch of kids, shortly out of high school, and with not much other than parties, beer, and girls on their minds.

I should add here, that I went in with my eyes wide open. I came to the fraternity looking for a party, and I found exactly what I was looking for. I wanted to be cool for a while. I wanted to be admired, respected, and most of all, loved, particularly by girls or at least one special girl. All my life, I had been an easygoing, kindhearted guy, but as the saying sometimes goes, nice guys finish last, and while there had only been a few girls in my life that I was interested in, they had never been interested in me.

I had been motivated to move out of my parent's house earlier that fall and down to the school by the loss of my first love. I met her the year before, my sophomore semester, sitting next to me in history class. I was nineteen and she was twenty-two. It started very simply, she sat down next to me and said hello. Within two weeks of class we were good friends and by the third week her presence had started to affect me. We studied together, talked on the phone, and something connected us deeply as friends. I looked up to her in so many ways. She was classy, confident, and had a very elegant way of carrying herself. Her hair was an almost white blonde and her eyes were a soft and tender sky blue. I truly cared for her with all my heart. Unfortunately, she was dating an older guy and simply didn't see me as anything more than a friend, a good guy, and "her little Oliver".

The semester I spent with her was the calm before the storm. I floated through my classes and everything in life seemed brighter and happier than any other time. We spent one semester of school together and then as smoothly as we met and became friends, she was gone. The force that orchestrates and choreographs our lives had brought us together for just a short time. The semester came to an end, and the last day of class marked the close of our meeting. I remember her last words. "I'll call you when I get back".

She never called, and if I try real hard, I can make out the image of a sunset. The sun's rays are glowing out of the ocean's waters as they disappear into the blue sea. The cloud's bellies are a soft pink as dusk moves in. It was after that heartbreak that I wanted to become someone else – someone the girls would love. Unrequited love, I would say, is possibly one of the most hurtful of human experiences. It causes us to question the very essence of who we are. While I had always hung out with a fairly cool group of guys, I, myself, never felt that cool. I was a star tennis player on the high school team and knew most everyone, but there was a shy and tender heart beneath the laughter and smiles.

After my sophomore year of college, I was out to obliterate the person I was as well as put an end to my pain and heart-ache. I ended up joining a fraternity in efforts to lose myself in beer and girls – and that's exactly what I did. My near perfect grades fell below passing during my pledging period. I was up most nights, drinking, partying, and always busy with the business of being cool. To be honest, at the time, it was just what I'd been seeking. It felt great to suddenly be given so much attention from girls and envy from other guys. The depression that had fallen over me due to love lost was blotted away, erased, or at least covered over for a while.

So this is who I was becoming as I went into the ritual. I was putting on a bit of a charade. Looking back, I wonder if the poor fellow was fighting for his life. As I see it, without the storm that was to come, I may have ended up the very person I secretly despised – vain, self-centered, sex and power driven, egotistical. And the saddest thing would have been that, inside, underneath the mask, I was actually the opposite of all those things.

The week before the initiation, I moved out of the dorms and into the old house I was living in with three other guys about five minutes from school. They were all pretty cool. We'd met at our fraternity house as pledges and had stuck together. The previous semester we'd been looking for a place and we finally found the dump we were living in. Basically, we wanted a place to party in. This house was right on the money, four bedrooms, two big open rooms, a pool table, and a huge back yard. It was all we needed.

We had barely moved in just before the initiation took place. The memory is hazy when I try to remember the particulars. Back then I couldn't have told you the exact date it happened. I guess it doesn't really matter, since I have *the journal*. Most of it is all there, the story that is. Now isn't the time to explain. What I need to tell you is that the journal was written ten years ago, after my fraternity initiation. I began writing it in response to a tremendous burst of creativity and desire to capture my experience on paper. In *A Dream is Born*, the journal begins by describing me sitting on the porch in the early morning hours. I am sitting outside my room at school and I am trying frantically to put my thoughts in order and understand just what happened the night before. I was dazed, confused, and very scared. I had gone outside to sit on my porch sometime during the night with the idea that everything would be better once the sun came up. I was literally waiting for the dawn. It is in this light that I now leave you with my story. Try to see through the haze as I did. Bit by bit, the journal most likely will do that for you, and footprint by footprint you will wander and walk the same dream which now seems so very long ago.

As I sit and write, I can tell you the day in question was Friday, January 24, 1992. All I should say is something went very wrong and life took a sudden and drastic turn. The turn was inward and it completely shattered the reality of the world in which I lived, as well as much of the one I still live in.

The journal was not at all an easy task to assemble, but I am now able to share it with you. Bit by bit was the way it came to me, and bit by bit is the way I give it to you.

In the Spirit of Love,

Oliver

Two

A Dream Is Born

Yesterday was pretty crazy. Or should I even call it yesterday? I guess that depends when I started writing? Yesterday was the 24th. The sun's kind, gentle, and soothing rays are finally climbing above the mountaintops overlooking the valley. Dawn has finally arrived on what seemed like the longest period of darkness I've ever experienced. It's really amazing just how slowly the night passes when you're not sound asleep in your bed, dreaming of tomorrow or yesterday, or whatever it is we dream about.

The night gave me a deep appreciation for the word darkness. There wasn't a cloud in the sky. The moon was nowhere to be found, and even the stars didn't seem to have their usual glimmer. It's as if time stopped or slowed just enough to throw the world off balance. Life has become deeply surreal, almost to the point where, for a while, I wondered if I'd been dreaming or imagining the whole night. It must be the haze. That's what I kept telling myself. "Just ride it out, Oliver; your mind is just confused and disoriented. Just wait till morning. Just wait till the sun comes up."

I haven't been feeling too well for a while now. Not just down, but strange. Kinda funny strange. Sometimes I feel real light and for some reason my eyes start to tear up. Other times there's an ache around my heart. I haven't really given it much thought, though. It's just something I've never felt before, as if all my emotions are intensified. I never questioned the meaning. This started a week ago, right after the ritual.

What sucks is I thought things would be great once we were initiated into the fraternity. Last semester was a whirlwind as a pledge. All the parties, drinking, loss of sleep, and existing on roll tacos at three in the morning really took a toll on me. I thought I'd be able to relax and have some peace now, but somewhere deep inside, I feel that I've really screwed things up badly this time. Call it intuition, but something is wrong; something inside has snapped or unleashed itself?

Yet I felt so perfect after the initiation, but that's when all this seemed to start. Maybe it is as powerful as they say? Maybe it does have some kind of magical power? All semester long I kept hearing how the ritualist had been some intellectual genius who had deeply studied the mystery schools and other esoteric rituals. It had taken many years of study and contemplation until he was able to form the ritual our fraternity holds so sacred.

It all seemed to be a bunch of hype that fit in all too nicely with the theme of being a pledge in a fraternity that fully endorsed the drug and party culture. They loved to play with our minds. Being a pledge pretty much consisted of a semester-long mental form of hazing in which a mystery or secret had to be discovered in order to reveal a Holy Grail of sorts.

I remember all those late nights at the frat house, without sleep, sitting for hours by a roaring fire, drenched in sweat, with only the flickering of flames providing light, and the crackling of logs intermixed with that crazy, almost haunting music playing over and over. And all those "pieces of the puzzle" they would read to us, like they were supposed to be some wisdom from the ages.

Maybe there was more to it? The brothers in the house kept telling us how the ritual would change our lives, make everything look brighter and purer, how we'd have more confidence and never be afraid of anything. That was all hype, right? The house is just a bunch of college kids, barely out of their teens, away from home, and trying their best to mess with our heads. I dismissed the whole semester as nothing more than a bunch of b.s. These guys didn't have any real knowledge or wisdom, all they did was drink, surf, and lounge around, without much purpose for that matter. The ritual had to be nothing more than the crowning glory to all the hazing.

But there was a change, almost immediately. I remember walking home, a newly initiated aspirant. I was completely high on life! I could have floated away in my glee, but the buzz only lasted an hour or so. After that, the bliss kind of came and went at different times throughout the days. It was so subtle I didn't question it, but now, it seems like a key piece to this mystery that consumes my thoughts. Just what happened to me? There really is a secret to unlock.

At first, the buzz felt so nice, I found myself writing poetry and words pretty much came effortlessly to my mouth. I was more confident, more at ease, and I seemed to have just the right things to say at the right moments. Why would I question anything like that? Life was looking just the way I wanted it to look. It seemed only natural that my happiness was the result of a high on life. Now I have to wonder?

With all the energy, I didn't need much sleep, and I stayed up most of the nights listening to love songs and writing poetry. God, why didn't I see this unfolding! That's insane for me to be indulging in that sap! Maybe that's what triggered this whole thing. Maybe I went and released all these feelings and emotions and they overwhelmed me. After all, it was only after a few days of the poems and love songs that the sadness started to come over me. That's when I'd find myself crying.

How in the world could I not see something was wrong when tears came to my eyes for no reason? Maybe I could have saved myself. Now, I don't even know what's happened; yet I feel as if my life depends on solving some mystery. Why didn't I pick up on any of these signs? Maybe the fog was already working on me, even though it wasn't thick enough to notice. There are just too many questions. Why did this happen? There has to be a cause and I have to find it, destroy it, and release myself. If not, if I can't solve this puzzle, I'm not sure how long I can take this.

Anyway, getting back to last night. Last night was a big party our frat has every semester. We met at school, where we hopped on a couple of old, rundown, greyhound buses that took us to the party. It's actually a pretty big affair, "Pref. Night". Every house on campus pairs up with a sorority. This year we had it at a bar on the bay, the Salmon House.

The ride down to the Salmon House was about thirty minutes. Fifteen minutes into the trip, I was sitting comfortably, watching the scenery go by, when a rush of blood flushed through my whole body causing a sharp tingling. I couldn't help but smile. I eased back into my seat and started chatting with a couple of young ladies as the now-familiar buzz descended upon me. I have no idea what they said, but I do know that whatever I said, we had a great conversation and I was more than charming.

I think that's what I like most about that feeling. Everything comes right from the heart. Words flow so smoothly. All of a sudden, a wall fades and I speak with pure emotion, and that emotion is actually contagious. It's not like it's a figment of imagination or delusions caused by a drug. There's so much loving energy flowing, I just can't contain it, and it kind of bubbles out. It's so infectious.

After thirty minutes I knew something wasn't quite right. All was not well. A week had passed since the ritual and I was more than acquainted with the occasional rush of emotion emerging and sloshing around within the walls of my mind, but the experience usually only lasted at most for twenty or twenty five minutes, and then the feeling would ebb and dissolve back into whatever pool it had emerged from. This time, however, instead of fading, the force appeared to be growing. An energy kept building, and then it became too intense. There must be some optimal level of peace, and wherever that level is, I passed right through it.

Upon realizing I was face to face with a force clearly more powerful than myself and growing bit by bit with each tick of time, I reacted with a hint of fear. Something was happening to me, I didn't know what, and this alone invoked a paralyzing dread. This wasn't going to be one of my better nights.

We'd already arrived at the bar. As I walked in, the lights played tricks. Strobes were flashing, the room was spinning, and brilliant colors or rainbows of light burst into awareness. I was more than a little scared. The chatty friend to all fell silent. Solitude was all I wanted; yet I was afraid to be alone. Fear quickly turned to panic, and in panic the door to the underworld cracked open.

This is where the night gets hazy. Smoke filled the bar while trancelike dance music blasted in rhythm on stage. Chaos appeared everywhere. So many people moving! Too much noise blaring! Confusion overwhelmed me as I became highly disoriented. Where were my buddies? Maybe they could calm me or at least help me in some way. Why was this happening? The more I thought, the more confused I got. My awareness crapped out, scattering within my head while my heart beat at a rate of frenzy fast enough to destroy the man of steel himself. Help!

Most of the crew were on the dance floor while a fog emerged and descended like a giant storm cloud concentrating all its fury on a single mountain peak, my mind. I stopped caring about the social aspect of the night. I wanted to survive. That's it, period. Dancing was the last thing on my mind so I decided to hang out where I was. Where I was, I'm not sure. Probably against the wall, which would have been holding me up.

How much time passed? I was slipping in and out of consciousness yet I must have been awake. More and more, the world resembled a dream. And then there was my heart, thumping harder and harder, and of course a whole lot faster still. Thoughts slipped beyond fear, rapidly moving toward craze. They were coming and going so ludicrously fast I had no chance of comprehending or deciphering even a jibber jabber.

Various things began flashing through my mind. Pictures, colors, tunnels, and swirling vortexes burst into vision. I just couldn't deal with any more information, whether it was from people talking, the lights, the noise, or anything even resembling some form of sensory input. My thoughts reached the speed of light. Even the slightest sights or sounds caused my body to shiver. Sudden laughter from the dance floor or the flash of a strobe light sent impulses running up my spine like electricity zipping through a time space continuum. My raw circuitry responded to every nuance, ever more sensitive to any form of input. Every second delivered still another jolt of energy. I couldn't take it anymore. Sensitivity was peaking and I started praying for some sort of release. The pain was too great. I had to escape somehow.

The party was in full swing. A few groups of people loitered around fringes of the packed dance floor, talking and laughing. Another fairly large group of people, mostly guys, were hanging out by the bar. This was obviously the less social group. These guys were on another plateau, the laid back of the earth, getting drunker and drunker, talking about surfing, beer, or things of that sort.

e

Watching and observing this scene, I remained in a daze, nothing more than a spectator as the night's events unfolded before me. Occasionally people would be in front of me. They would be moving their lips, talking, but it was as if they were ghosts. I didn't know what the hell they were saying. I didn't know what the hell they were doing. From their side of the coin, in the circle that I was loosely a part of, my behavior probably didn't seem too unusual. They most likely assumed I was high on some hallucinogen.

It's strange, while all this was going on, I clearly remember - when, I don't know - someone special was talking to me. I was on the pay phone over in the corner by the front doors. The call was definitely important, because I remember running around begging for a quarter. It took me one hell of a long time to get that quarter! It's only 25 cents for Christ's sake! Maybe I was so completely gone that no one could understand me. I think I might have finally found it myself. That or someone finally felt generous. Either way, I got it.

What a blur! I really can't say exactly what the call was about. There was the feeling of love pulsing through my body with every swish of my heart. Emotion was flowing like a river, straight from deep inside my chest, up my neck and into my throat where it all seemed to form a ball. If it grew any larger, I think I would have choked.

Words were spilling from my mouth. What were they? It's as if they didn't require any conscious thought or use of the mind. They bubbled straight from my heart and ended spilling into the phone like a waterfall.

When I found myself on the phone, I had already crossed the line; I was in the abyss. I had no control over what I was saying or what I was doing. My deepest instinct had taken over, stepped into my head, and started with its own agenda, pure emotion, not even a hint of anything else.

I've never had much control of this chariot of emotion that

was using the phone. Every once in a while, a part of me gets out of its cage and oozes out all kinds of soft and poetic-like babble. And as I stood there on the phone, clinging to the last strands of sanity, this piece of me not only escaped, but also took full control of the reigns. Add to that, I couldn't have cared any less. One hundred percent of my efforts were concentrated on living. I didn't have time or the presence of mind to be tugging on the reins of an obviously out of control pair of horses. The truth is, I think they knew this all too well. It was now or never. Their time had finally come, and to be honest, they weren't wasting any of it.

And this person on the phone? Who was I talking to? I could have done some really permanent damage to the old rep. Oh why couldn't I have remembered that at the time? Any ego dwelling in me blacked out when all the hysteria kicked in. I was in a battle for life and ego was nowhere in sight. In fact, maybe a good sized piece of ego passed away in those moments. I know whoever was on the other end will never think of me the same again, but it just doesn't matter.

The sun is pretty high in the sky now.

I wish I could know whom I was speaking with? That really puzzles me because I remember a few things. One is, I'm pretty sure - positive actually - I was speaking with someone feminine. Murphy's Law. Another is, I might have said I was about to die, and I was explaining that I had to say, "I love you" before I did. It's not much considering I was on the phone for quite a while. The whole thing is rather baffling, but it's got to hold a key to this puzzle.

I guess I got a little off track. Back to the club. I was standing by the corner exit of the bar. When? Other than arriving and a few other moments, there is simply no time line. Maybe it was before I was on the phone, maybe it was after. Maybe I'll never know. Panic and fear were peaking. A whirling sound spun through my head and the room vanished. A jolt shot up my spine and I lost feeling in my hands and legs. My body started to tingle. Just when I thought I was having a heart attack or a stroke, something snapped. I felt a rip just below my ribs. I blacked out for a second or two. There was the feeling of falling. In the next instant, I was numb. The panic was gone; the fear was gone. Just emptiness. No relief, no pain. Emotion was nonexistent. I seemed to be merely an observer of myself. The music still blasted and screams filled the air, yet there was a deep sense of silence. Sounds of laughter and music were merely a faint rumble in the background.

I scanned the room, taking in everything visually. Not a single, solitary thought ran through my head. Only visual sights and sounds remained as I soaked in the environment. A crowd gathered. People were flailing in some kind of panic.

Someone was yelling as he shoved the guy standing next to me.

"Call an ambulance!"

In that moment, I must have gained some sense because I asked what had happened. Maybe no one heard me but another body came running over. I've never seen such chaos! Through the haze I made out crowds of people. They seemed to be speaking all at once. Their words swirled together and became one muffled, gurgled, groaning noise, and then I was numb again. Life seemed so quiet? I was utterly unattached to the whole situation. I just watched without thinking. The strobe lights no longer had any effect on me. I was hollow. Time was gone.

The crowd moved from the bar to the front parking lot, and I went right along. I couldn't get a look at exactly what was happening but apparently someone was hurt. Normally I would have been deeply concerned, but this time emotion didn't have any bite. I was dead inside, lifeless. Some kind of trance had settled on me. The silence was profound. Time passed, and although something terrible was happening, I felt no pain.

A low scream grew louder and louder in the distance as it traveled towards us. Soon I recognized the siren of an ambulance. Perhaps five minutes passed and I caught sight of a paramedic van. The sirens screeched their loudest as it turned the corner and made its way toward the crowd.

For some reason, when the ambulance pulled up, I felt a surge of fear tear through the nothingness. It didn't last long or feel anything like the panic I'd felt earlier, more of a quick breeze of fear that blew past me and then all fell silent once again.

Off in the distance, about fifty yards away, the ambulance came to a stop, and its siren finally ceased. The flashing red lights still remained and the sudden absence of the sirens' call made the night grow quieter still. All my attention focused on the red light, every drop, and the rest of the night was obliterated. Within seconds, the lights produced a hypnotic daze comprised of nothing but itself. I didn't quite notice the attendants get out and rush towards the commotion. I didn't quite notice the stretcher wheeling from the ambulance. I didn't notice much of anything.

As seamlessly as it arrived, the ambulance pulled away and sirens started singing. They faded as the ambulance moved farther and farther away - which makes sense - but the sirens became more and more melodic. Something about their whine caused them to pass from the realm of noise to music, only adding to a surreal calm all around. The music filled my ears long after the ambulance disappeared. I wonder if I was imagining the sounds because they lingered for so long. Perhaps it was because my sense of time was corrupted? Eventually, the sweet call of the sirens disappeared into the silence of the night.

Similar to the moment when a fever starts to break, there was a noticeable physical relief. As the ambulance pulled away,

I closed my eyes after possibly the worst night of my life and imagined myself back at home, tucked into my bed, all wrapped in warm covers, staring up at the beautiful tapestry above my bed. I felt the same as the dying of the winds and rain in the eye of a powerful storm. The winds calmed and the rain subsided along with the fear, almost to the point where one might wonder what all the worry was about?

I have no idea how I made it home but I guess that's not too amazing, definitely not a first. My eyes ached from all the lights back at the bar so I didn't want any bright lights on in my room. Instead, I plugged in my black light. It's much softer on the eyes, and once the light turned on, the whole room came alive with colors. I decorated it just so it would have this effect. It's not too big of a room, maybe ten by fifteen, and its walls are wood panels. On the side connecting to the main house, about three feet in, there's a counter top about a foot and a half wide. It looks like a bar but it's really an addition some other tenant built. The room really isn't supposed to be a room, more of sunroom, and I guess somebody built the bar to use as a funky closet.

In between the closet and the house is a sliding glass door that leads to a deck. The glass has been blacked out with dark paper and the bar-closet only takes up three quarters of the width. That leaves about three feet of sliding glass door leading to the house. I like the way the black paper covering the glass door looks, so I bought a bunch of giant black sheets and covered the other three walls completely. The carpet is some really cheap, shorthaired stuff, all in light beige. My bed is a queen-sized futon, and it's on the floor in the far corner, parallel to the bar. That leaves about four feet in between the bar and the foot of my bed. In that space, I have a very old fashioned desk the other tenant left behind. I think it's some kind of wood, maybe maple. There are no drawers, just four legs, a flat top, and a matching chair. It's stained a rich, deep, reddish brown.

The sheets on my futon glow when the black light hits them. They're dark teal blue with tiny splotches of black speckled throughout. It's almost like someone splattered black paint on top of a rich teal blue canvas. It gives off a calm and soothing feel.

What really lights up the room is the monstrous sheet I have hanging above the bed. It covers the entire ceiling and I tacked it up with a nail in each corner so it hangs down in the middle. It's definitely a professionally done tapestry and it has to be filled with every color imaginable. Little bits and pieces of dots and color all work together in different designs and flowing shapes.

When I stumbled hazily into my room and I plugged in the light, the illusion created overwhelmed me. With the black light on, the bed and tapestry came to life, while the rest of the room disappeared into black nothingness. The effect was enchantingly surreal. The lights alone could have sent anyone into an altered state.

I didn't see it at the time but last night made a few things clear. I was really heading down the wrong roads. Maybe last night was just a swift kick in the ass from God himself? When I have time, I think I'll tear down all the sheets and crap and let the sun in again. After all, it was a sun room to begin with.

By the way, it's turned into a beautiful day. There is a mist coming up over the hills and the sun's rays have just the right amount of warmth.

Once I flipped on the black lights, the room cast its spell and the haze thickened. What a crazy night! Finally I could let go and find some peace. I felt so safe in my room. I lay down on my bed and bundled myself up tight, wrapped in covers. It was pretty cold, and since there isn't much insulation with the room being built on top of the porch overhang, I felt really cold. Shivery cold. All snug in covers, I felt like a big ice cube slowly melting. The contrast was so soothing and my body was tingling, ever more relaxed with every sensation. The sheet hanging from the ceiling was glowing like a red-hot poker.

Watching the different colors in the sheet radiating so intensely was amazing. All the little dots seemed to take their own personality. Looking back, it seems that I was watching for hours. Maybe I was. I was on my back with my head gently nestled between three pillows, two small ones on the sides and the big one spread across like a big sandwich. I didn't really feel tired, more mesmerized than tired. I could actually pick out any single dot of color on the sheet, and as I kept my attention on it, it came to life. The colors were intense to begin with, but as I focused on one speck, it seemed to increase in brilliance. The other colors would blur then fade, and then, when I couldn't hold my gaze anymore, they would all return, each with their own color and shape.

I kept repeating the experience over and over. My consciousness expanded and contracted while the tapestry's hypnotic spell wove around me. The world outside was too quiet? No sound of cars passing by on the streets. No cries of laughter from one of the neighbors having a party. It still wasn't that late, probably 11:30 or so. There should have been some kind of noise.

Between the quiet, the pitch-black room, and the black light that was bringing the sheet perched above me to life, the painting came together to form what will probably end up being the most surreal moment of my life. Every cell in my body was dripping with anesthesia. Whom can I give credit for the moment? My mind screeched to a halt. I don't know if I could say my name. I don't even know if I knew my name! No thoughts seemed to be forming and the haze transformed into a dense fog that seemed to envelope everything from my eyes up. I was as dumb as a rock, too dumb to realize I was being lulled out of my senses.

I picked a spot right in the middle of the sheet. It was one of the smaller splotches of color and was completely white. The pattern was tougher to pick out, probably because it was so small, like a pinpoint, and because all the other colors were so intense and seemed to draw me in on their own. This one I had to search for. In fact, it was so small, at first, I didn't think I could keep my eyes focused on it. But like the other colors, once I concentrated, its glow increased and all else softly faded. Usually my gaze would shift and the whole landscape would return, but a few times my attention held a bit longer until the light merged with the darkness in the room. Except for the glowing white speck I was fixed on, I would have been in total darkness.

I remember being extremely impressed with the illusion, and as I lost my grip on the white point of light, I realized there were millions of other glimmering lights, some extremely brilliant, and others barely visible. A cold air engulfed me and for an instant I was outside looking up at a moonless night completely blanketed in stars.

There is only one other time in my life when I've seen a sky as impressive and that was when I was camping in the desert out in Joshua Tree. I couldn't believe how sharp and crystal clear a night sky could be. Quite a few people had telescopes. I remember looking at the night sky while I lay in my sleeping bag pondering how limitless the universe was. My imagination couldn't begin to capture the sheer size of life.

For just a few seconds, I thought I actually was back at Joshua Tree, staring up at the stars. That would have made me eighteen. I remembered all my hopes and dreams, and for that moment, I was there in the desert, eighteen years old, and reliving the whole thing.

I grew up in a world created completely in its own vacuum. Life was fair and kind, and in the end everything always worked out. Anything was possible and I felt the special-ness everyone feels at a young age. Maybe that was my well of self-worth. I was taught about right and wrong, and all the movies, fairytales, and images that created my world spoke of goodness and love triumphing, always. I believed with all my heart and there was simply no room for doubts. How could I doubt? Everything that came into my world fit perfectly into the story. The story was a fairytale and I had no reason to doubt that life was a fairytale.

My world was safe and magical with no imperfection. I was a genuinely nice kid. I grew up in a small city in San Diego where there was not much to worry about. A big day for the local sheriff was if they caught an extra kid or two speeding.

When we first moved there it was more of a large town, with rolling hills and cows grazing. Most homes had a good size yard, and many people had a horse or two. There was a golf course where we lived and the city had a beautiful lake surrounded by mountains and a freshly trimmed grass meadow where you could sit and enjoy the peace of the landscape. I spent many days fishing at the lake and communing with nature. It wasn't until years later that Poway became a big suburb, with malls, movies, and all the bells and whistles of any modern day city. Now the cows are gone and there are apartments and stores everywhere.

My parents were two of the most loving people you could ever meet. We weren't rich, but we had enough money to live in a nice house and enjoy the good things in life without struggling too much, pretty much like most upper-middle class families in the seventies and eighties.

My dad had been a great athlete in his life, getting a scholarship to college for basketball and going on to graduate from law school. His parents were Armenians, both escaping from the country during the invasion by the Turkish from 1915 – 1918. His mother's parents were killed and she escaped to France with the neighboring family when she was about six. She later made her way to the United States via Cuba where she met my grandfather. In an amazing coincidence, he was also from the same village as her and had found eventual refuge in the U.S. They had two kids, Sara and John, my dad.

Mom was an adventurous woman, born in Germany during the war. She planned to travel the world working on a cruise ship as an activities director. She traveled to many countries and she came to America when she was twenty-one to fine tune her English. She then met my dad at a resort in Miami and soon made a very courageous decision to leave her homeland and family at only twenty-two and marry my father. She, too, was very close to her family with an older brother whom she adored as well as a very creative and artistic sister to inspire her.

Family was the center of our lives, and my parents, both whom had become successful after growing up in poverty, tried to give me and my sister whatever could possibly make us happy. Much of our time was spent at the neighborhood county club where I would play tennis all day while my sister might spend time at the pool with her friends. She was a great big sister, always kind enough to let me play with her and her friends when they were over. They'd give me some little job to keep me included and that made me happy. As we got older, she emerged as the more social, hanging out with a popular crowd, going to all the dances and all the little social activities at school. While I wasn't a big talker, she was talking all the time! Introvert and Extrovert - no question at all.

I'm fairly smart, so you'd think that I would have done well in school but grades and homework were low on my list. I spent all my time playing sports and just having fun. I had the brains, but seldom used them when it came to class. My sister was an overachiever to my underachiever. She squeezed her brain for all it was worth and ended up at UCLA where she did very well, eventually going on to law school at USD.

Growing up, I spent some of the greatest hours of my life playing tennis with my dad. He loved his kids and our joy was his joy. Later, when I started to get pretty good, we would travel all around southern California, and I would play different regional tennis matches. We had a great time together, always enjoying the experience, not so much whether I won or lost. My dad never showed any sign of disappointment if I lost a match. He just wanted me to do my best and whatever happened was fine. Although I lacked the killer instinct that many of the best players seemed to have, I was fortunate enough to inherit some of my dad's athletic skills, and I did become a top ranked tennis player in southern California. This was very good for me as a source of confidence and self-discipline, especially since I was rather sensitive and a bit shy sometimes.

My friends were also athletes and they ranged the entire spectrum of personalities. We had the comedians, the cools guys, the intelligent, and the mischievous – an overall good-hearted collection of guys, not too bad and not too good either. We had our fun, ditching classes occasionally and giving a teacher or two a hard time. I was always smiling, laughing, and pretty much having a good time. Not much bothered me and I got along with most everyone.

If I had a weakness, it was with the girls. Everything else came easily and seemed to go my way. I was interested only occasionally but usually I would keep my feelings to myself. At the same time, something deep inside assured me that one day I would meet a wonderful woman and she would take a long look at my heart and fall madly in love. My parents loved each other deeply and I never heard them say an unkind word to each other or even raise their voices. That's what I understood marriage to be.

So I grew up in this fairytales always have happy endings life and I have to say, it was a rather joyous existence. Of course, as I grew up, the world I lived in was challenged now and then. Although my life seemed so perfect, I realized others were suffering. Terrible things were happening all over the world. Why all the hurt and pain? I had to have answers because logic told me if others suffered, then maybe the world I lived in was more fragile than I realized. Maybe life wasn't really a fairytale always with a happy ending?

I turned to God and Spirit for answers. I attended church a few times when I was very young and I found myself dusting off a bible given to me my first day at Sunday school. I found solace in the Love of Light. I had to be very creative about my reading, always reading between the lines. The bottom line I came to; Christ was teaching about love. He showed us how to become more loving creatures through self-love and love of others. Christ told us that if we followed his example, love would unlock the door to great treasures that lay within us all. I concluded Christ actually only spoke of love, and I reasoned he came to free us from our self-created suffering. People had forgotten about true love and lost touch with the deeper part within.

What I was left with turned out to be the foundation my world, fantasyland, was built upon. I thought the suffering in the world was caused by our own ignorance of the God within. Eventually, a time would come when we all wake to this realization, and bit-by-bit, the world would reflect the heavens, which were filled with love. In the heavens, souls were awake to their divine origin and love and peace were everywhere. If only the earth could awaken to that reality, then heaven on earth would be possible. Christ remembered where he came from and told of his kingdom so the earth could make her ascent. "On earth as it is in heaven".

I knew Christ and so many other wonderful people who chose to come to the earth had done so in their desire to enlighten those who walked the earth. In fact, I reasoned that everyone, to his own degree, was here to grow in love and compassion, moving closer to heaven. All living things had their divine place, and in the end, when our time on earth ended, our destiny would be revealed and we would understand how holy and blessed the earth was for our presence. It was the perfect ending, and it allowed me to believe in Camelot.

The problem was that Camelot was beginning to be attacked. The world around me simply didn't reflect the heavens and some of the things I believed in began to crumble. I sought refuge by withdrawing into myself a bit. I lived in songs and in poetry. I lived at the lake fishing or in the mountain wind. I lived with the eagles and nature itself. I immersed myself in great novels and plays. I laughed and danced to the most inspirational and joyous songs and music. I walked the sands by the ocean and silently flew over the waters and balanced on the edge of waves. My inner world grew more and more brilliant and magical with each passing day.

The world I lived in had been loosely grounded in reality, but the attacks actually made Camelot even more brilliant, until its riches and splendor were of another realm. I realized Camelot lived between the lines, like in a poem. It couldn't be touched or seen too easily, but it was all around me. The most talented artists paint Camelot. The inspired poets and writers tell stories of Camelot. The genius musicians write anthems about Camelot. We all work to create Camelot and then somehow dismiss it as being nothing more than imagination. Imagination is the very tool that has sculpted Camelot! It is the fabric that paints the streets!

Camelot is where I lived, in peace, and always with hope. Bit by bit, I was choosing a different world to live in. Unfortunately, another part of me simply couldn't escape. After all, I was flesh and blood and I lived in the real world, not in some story, or poem, or even a song for that matter. I didn't have that luxury. I lived in reality, and that teacher began to hammer its lesson home.

I knew people get jaded and I looked at all the people who were pissed off about life, totally unhappy, and I decided I just wasn't going to become that way. I'd fight with all my heart. I didn't realize it, but I'd created my own little war.

At eighteen, I sat staring up at the stars above Joshua Tree, thinking about love and life. Now I cringe because I know between that day and twenty, the rains and floods descended upon my treasured city like never before. I knew the final blow to my heart would be too much. My heart would break over another girl who preferred a cool guy to a nice guy. What would kill me is that she was the one, the one that was supposed to see the beauty inside me and fall in love. Camelot would fall and be erased from memory. I have so much love and compassion for that poor kid who was unaware of the coming storm.

In the next instant I gained my wits and the stars in the sky began vanishing, almost as if someone was blotting out each speck of light. Momentum increased and the night collapsed into itself. For an instant I was incased in a darkness completely devoid of light, just a flash, and then the faint, blurred outline of shapes filled with light came into sight.

I stared into the wonderful white light above, followed by the return of all the other colors until I was gazing up at a sheet. My senses returned and I understood I'd been staring at the tapestry above me the whole time.

It's an illusion I love. I love the way my mind couldn't

comprehend what was happening. I went through this fading in and out of worlds. It became a game. The glowing white dot in the middle of the sheet would slowly suck my awareness inward until I briefly lost myself and found I was outside marveling at the night sky. The illusion held itself together for mere seconds, but somehow time expanded. I relived so many memories of past in those instants. Experiences lasting several days were completely relived in a second. Feelings from so long ago surfaced, reminding me of who I once was. There is simply no explanation for the twisting of time. When I would snap back into my room, I'd realize I'd been gone for just moments, but when lost in the illusion, it seemed to last forever.

Each time I returned to the room, it was a little easier to drift away. I found the time spent in my room decreasing while the time in illusion increased. How many times did I bounce between these two worlds? I really can't say because the experience was so hypnotic. I must have drifted off to sleep. How long I was asleep is tough to tell as well. So many tricks played in my mind. It could have been for a fraction of a second, hours, or maybe even days.

When I gained awareness, I was in the middle of what can only have been a dream. I was awake, yet my senses provided no information or clues to my condition. Perhaps I was in the state of mind just before we wake up or just before drifting off into sleep. I tried to move, but thoughts had no effect on my limbs.

I slipped into the same tranquil state I'd experienced earlier. Energy pulsated. I could easily hear my heart thumping as it pumped blood, getting more intense with every squeeze. A sweet morphine flowed through my veins. My body easily accepted the waves of warmth that washed over every cell. I noticed my breathing was imperceptible. A deeper and greater peace bubbled within.

It wasn't long before I lost myself in this bliss. Somewhere in the middle of nothingness, I was floating, weightless. A sort of pleasant chatter was washing through me. I was laughing. It wasn't quite me though. I was four of five at the most, a little kid laughing with all my heart. Something was speaking to me! Whatever it was, no words were used. I don't think it was telepathy either. In telepathy, I think you understand what the other person is saying. What was happening was more of a communion with an intelligent vibration. It was telling me jokes, jokes about life and the funny things that go on on earth. Life was suddenly hilarious. I was laughing and laughing while this loving presence kept telling me the funniest stories.

I heard myself speaking. My voice was of a young child filled with so much excitement the mouth can't contain it. The child was in heaven, in ecstasy.

"You're funny!"

I can't write the answer because there is no way to write what I felt, and I don't even know what message was returned. All I know is the communion continued and I grew more and more ecstatic and happy. A light and heat approached, closer and closer. The closer I got, the more lost in bliss I became. Hurricane force energetic power flowed within me. I could do anything! Closer and closer. I could barely control myself! I was magic; miracles were possible! The light penetrated my soul, moving through me as if I were transparent. Whatever I believe will become reality! The sense of my body was dissolving.

I heard myself speaking with childlike wonder and amazement. "Are you God?" There was no reply. The same loving presence somehow conveying joy and bliss kept emanating. Light flashed through me as wind impervious to any structure. I was light itself! I couldn't turn around; I had no more will to resist the light's temptation. I couldn't move, couldn't speak, couldn't manage to wipe the smile from what I perceived as my face! I was too ecstatic to think! The pleasure was too great!

"He is at the very gates."

I clearly heard the voice. Did it come from the light? Peaceful, loving, and gentle, it seemed a different voice, speaking in my own timber, not as a child anymore, definitely an adult. The voice was smooth and crisp, causing me to think of something very old and wise. Yet it was a part of me. It came from somewhere deep within.

"You know you died tonight."

The words were without emotion but they hit their mark with tremendous force.

"What do you mean, I died tonight? I'm not dead." I was more confused than scared.

"You died tonight. You are not breathing. Your heart is not beating."

Again the words, peaceful and calm, but without a hint of excitement. The voice seemed to be my own, only more confident and exact. Each word was carefully chosen and spoken with a caring concern, but very matter-of-factly. I felt like a child gently being told the family pet had just expired.

No question about it, I was being handled like a delicate flower. It wasn't so much in the words as it was in the tone of the voice. Add to that, it was somehow my own voice. Every sense told me I was listening to myself. Not like the way I normally think though. It was literally like putting on some headphones and listening to a tape of myself talking. The tone was non-wavering. It was ever so gentle.

My impression was this voice knew everything about me and so much more. I was merely a small piece of the whole, a subset of something greater. The conversation was between child and father or maybe brother and big brother. The big brother understood what was happening and what was going to happen. He had already traveled the path and knew what lay ahead. It's the only way I can figure the voice could have been so serene and caring as it delivered the message.

I checked for my breath, and there was none. I wasn't breathing! Every cell started screaming with agony. "No! No! No! I can't die! I can't die!" I was trying to mentally run and escape the impending doom revealed to me.

"No! My family, my parents, my friends, my . . ." I wasn't rational anymore. Thoughts were pure emotion. My only concern was the pain I would cause those I loved so much. I couldn't let their love for me betray them. I would not betray them. I would fight hell for an eternity to remain in their presence. "No! I'm not dead! I won't die. Oh God, no! Please God, help me! Please God! Please God, my life is yours, just let me return! I will live just for those I love! I give up my life! Please God, save me! Save me!"

The tender voice spoke again. The peace of the voice washed over me, and in that instant, everything was perfect. Whatever the voice said was pure gold. I wasn't dead. I wasn't going to die. Peace and love were everywhere. In those seconds I passed through perfection, perfection beyond mind.

I never knew what it's like to have a single thought and nothing else to hold on to. It's so quiet.

"You are going to fight a great battle."

The voice again, it brought sanctuary. No thoughts other than the calm, soothing voice were permitted to enter. They would have their turn, but for the moment, all was calm.

"You have traveled deep into the depths and you will make a great journey. You will search heart and soul and must cross the distance between mind and heart. I will cover up the memory because it will have been too painful for you. The path you have traveled is a rocky one, but one that leads to light. Many doors have been shut in the great mansion and many others have been opened. You have passed through these doors and through these doors you must pass once more.

31

You will not have passed through every room when you will find the door you are seeking.

"Your mind has been laid in siege, and the senses in your body have grown dull. Spirit will be tested, but it is your heart that will lead your footsteps, for in the fifth castle one thinks with his heart alone.

"Once redeemed, you will be free, yet you will have a purpose and a path to follow. Hold it close to your heart. Your prayers are always heard, and they are answered. Angels protect you, and spirit will guide you. Always lead with your heart, and follow the light. The mind holds you captive where its vipers make you ill and their words lead you astray. In the inner mansion you will be safe from the mind's simple demons that distract and confuse. Until then you must listen for your heart and follow your beliefs and ideals.

"Before you find the door, all the fury of the mind will rise up to prevent extinction. These are the deeper teachings of hurt and pain where all your power has been held captive in false memories and emotions that only the subconscious is capable of holding onto with such ferocity. They will be uprooted and released into the nothingness from which they came. They have no power except the power you have given them. You will search all areas for the hurtful seeds that have been planted and grown. They sought to destroy you from within. It has been said by the Great Master, 'Not a stone shall be unturned'.

"Once the mind has been freed, life will once again be filled with light, for there will only be sun. I smile because I know this will be so. You will win this battle."

I can't remember it now, but in those moments of bliss, I too knew the ending. I heard myself speaking and I knew why I sounded so loving and sure of myself.

"Tonight you have been given a great gift. Where the heart and love are involved mettle can be turned to gold. Never doubt this has been a gift. Humbly receive it, for there will be times when you will want to curse what you have found tonight only as others beg for the teaching.

"Always love, with all your soul for that matter. You are never alone and never will be. Life is a precious gift! In the hardest times, envision the ending. Picture it in your mind, imagine it, shape it, nurture it. It is yours to create. Follow these truths and in the end, you will look back upon life and have no regrets, only loving memories."

As the voice finished speaking, the light increased and intensified until I was once again lost in the light. I floated higher and higher, feeling more and more filled with energy. Waves of communication washed over me, and I was once again a child, laughing and giggling at the funny things I was being told. A thought exploded into my head as if someone had planted a bomb and lit the fuse.

"Do you want to write this down?"

"Yeeaaaaahhhhh!" I was speaking in the voice of a child. I screamed the answer with glee as the bomb kept going off in my head over and over.

"Do you want to write this down? Do you want to write this down? Do you want to write this down?"

The thought consumed me so intensely I had to be writing at that very instant. A second later wouldn't do. There was a whoosh sound and I faintly heard my own, calm, loving voice, saying, "You are going to wake up now."

I was outside staring up at a night sky filled with thousands of stars looking down upon me. I took a deep breath of the night air and gazed upward toward thousands of tiny specks of color, all glowing, radiating a spectrum of light. In the next instant, the walls around me returned, encasing the illusion while revealing I was lying in my bed, merely staring at the sheet above me. The black light had the room looking rather suspect, a bit too surreal and dreamy. Was I still asleep?

From the deep caverns of a well, the biggest urge to write flooded my heart. I opened the door from my room leading to the side deck. I flicked on the porch light.

The wood was creaking and moaning as I walked around the corner to the overhang that looks down into the yard. I leaned against the railing and looked up to the heavens. The ever so faint gray night gave enough light to see the silhouette of huge bushes and plants in the yard. Why was existence still so quiet?

Amazingly, I found my favorite gray sheepskin jacket I'd lost. I wrapped it around me and leaned back into the chair on the porch and put my feet on the deck railing. A cold chill in the air really kept me awake. I thought I'd be up for a couple of hours until I got tired. As it turned out, I've been up all night.

It wasn't long before my mind started playing. Every last bit of fear and worry or hurt came after me during the darkness. Mean things I said when I was a kid. Mean things other kids said to me. Stupid things I'd said, stupid things I've done. All the times my feelings got hurt, all the times I'd hurt others. Basically, all the crap that had ever entered my mind decided to revolt and attack me.

The night was so long. Sometimes delusions would come after me in the form of hallucinations and other times I would feel myself crying as emotions bubbled up from some place within. I re-experienced so many painful events and relived so many crazy times. Sometimes it would just be voices in my head arguing with each other. Anger, hate, sadness. They were all there. It all came out, especially the anger, so many things eventually lead to anger or hurt. I found that out very quickly.

How long the night truly was I don't know, but I sat in the darkness and it took every ounce of strength I had to survive. Time was bent and twisted so it wouldn't be fair to judge the darkness by a clock. I do know I sat here on the porch for most of the night, waiting. I figure it's the sun I was waiting for, that somehow, when the first rays of light came flooding down the mountain, they would wash away all my fear and confusion. I started writing just before the sun came up. This overpowering impulse to write won't leave me alone.

Thank God for the daylight. Now at least I know things are going to be ok, that the sun did rise, that life will go on. For a bit there, I actually thought I had gone crazy, or better put, in my craziness, I thought I'd slipped into some pizzaro type of world; a world of darkness where all my fears lived and breathed as real as reality itself.

All night long, as I was praying for some relief, some speck of hope, I kept expecting some mutants of horror to jump out and attack me in the worst imaginable ways. It was as if a door had opened, and all my fears and fantasies came flooding through the valley all at once. My body was paralyzed by fear, and my mind kept moving faster and faster, running from fear, running from itself. I didn't move or make a sound, but anyone who could have seen my eyes would have known that although I was completely motionless and silent, inside, I was a lunatic. The eyes would definitely have given me away. My pupils were severely dilated and they were soaking up whatever light there was in the sky. They had to look like the eyes of a crazed cat, glowing in the dark.

At times I became a bystander to what was going on inside my head. During these times I reminded myself that in the morning things would be much better. I had to fight through waves of panic and fear. Panic that I was dying, that I wasn't breathing, that time was critical, that I wasn't going to live.

I still feel really strange. The sun's been up for a while now and it's all I can do to stay awake. I don't think I've been to sleep yet. It's hard to say, I can't tell if it was a dream I had, or some kind of waking hallucination? The whole night is becoming more and more like a dream to me, it's so hard to remember?

My last clear memory is being in the dance club, freaking out, and then hearing that popping sound, feeling some type of rip. After that, things get too hazy. There are also large periods blocked out of memory, portions of time that are missing. Those missing pieces must hold some clues to this puzzle? The longer I go without writing this down, the less I will remember. Of that much I'm positive. It's like this fog bank blows in, softening memories until the past becomes a hazy dream.

I'm going to write as much as I can remember. One day I'll read this and be so grateful I captured the moment. This is one dream that won't be lost to the mist.

Three

LIGHTING OF THE SACRED FIRE

I slept the deepest sleep of my life. No dreams. No waking in the middle of the night. No worries, no nothing. An hour after I finished writing yesterday, I crawled back into my bedroom, turned off the black light, and immediately fell into a sleep rivaling Rip Van Winkle in his most somber moments. My senses had ridden the rapids far longer than design permits and ultimately plunged over the falls, utterly and totally exhausted. After waking from the rest that only the sleep of oblivion could possibly provide, I think I'm going to be ok. I'm doing so much better.

Once I began to stir from my extended nap, I cautiously raised my eyelids. Honestly, I was in great fear of what I might see. I pictured myself in a coma, lying paralyzed in some hospital bed with tubes filled with various fluids dripping into me. So much haze and disoriented thoughts had passed through my head, how could I be sure of anything? It took some time to gather a few grains of courage, but really, there was no turning back. Open they flopped, and then it was official; I was safe in my room, all bundled in warm covers and tucked in my beautiful little bed. I stayed for at least a few hours, relaxing, remembering, and attempting to assemble the various pieces of whatever actually took place. It's all a blur. Thank God for the journal. Without yesterday's entry, I wouldn't have anything to grab on to. All that craziness I wrote is spellbindingly unbelievable. In fact it is. It must be. It's just imaginary babble produced by a crazed mind, but for some reason, it's all I can think about? I'm obsessed. Nothing else matters and I'm tormented by an emptiness that's complete and unrelenting.

The remainder of the day was spent reading. I read that journal over and over and still over again, trying to come up with some meaning, some kind of sensible answers. There're so many clues, yet I grasp nothing. There are no footholds and this burning desire to understand the night haunts me. Some kind of message is contained within the mist and haze, hidden like some grail or elixir that holds the power of life and death. The quest consumes me to my core, charring all I once held dear.

It's actually quite frightening, not being able to remember a portion of time, a portion of life. What did I say to people? Did I say any mean things? After all, I had no control, not a drop. I wish I could beam myself into the ether and pop out in the future a few weeks from now when I've forgotten the whole stupid night. Then this horror will be over and things will be the way they were.

I just wish I wasn't so paranoid. Every nook and cranny of my flesh is drenched in anxiety, even my bones, especially right in the middle of my chest. I've got all this nervous energy pushing, pulling, and dripping into my blood, poisoning my thoughts. Every synapse is soaked in the thick muck of misery.

The body out of balance is a horrible experience. Hell really. Especially when the cause of the disharmony is mental. Once the delicate chemistry of the brain breaks down, everything falls apart. Restlessness, agitation, anxiety - they are all like some kind of slow water torture unleashed and set in motion by forces that seem to arise from utter chaos. Sitting still for even short moments simply wasn't possible. Restlessness forced me to spring to my feet or spontaneously shift into another posture. Once standing, I'd get so anxious I had to sit down! Every fuse was blown! My entire circuitry was screwed up! One minute I'd be so tired and dizzy I had to lie down, only to be assaulted with a blitz of prickling, pulsating electricity until I retreated right back to where I'd started a few seconds earlier.

I ended on the balcony the rest of the day, just like yesterday, only I wasn't writing like a madman. I sat in different positions trying Jedi mind tricks to tune out and ignore the aches and haywire impulses bouncing through my body. Is there any way to fight the sensations? They're constantly with me, laughing and teasing. The best I can do is ignore them, kind of a learned helplessness of sorts. Like a rat in an electric cage, I am stuck inside my broken body until I get better, until something changes. That's what makes it a bit easier though, time will fix what's wrong. Another good night sleep and I'll be ten times better. I obviously shocked my system, but life will work itself out.

With no one home, the house is so quiet. Birds sing in the yard, wind rustles through leaves, and occasionally a dog barks out, but a serene, calm silence, is always the undertone. I've been searching the silence for lost pieces of time, lost pieces I fear will never be recovered. I'm sorting through the rubble, looking for hints of meaning. Call it curiosity but I have to solve a puzzle. What happened? What did it mean? Maybe it meant nothing. Maybe, but I keep returning and returning to the pages I wrote yesterday. My desire to catch a glimmer of an explanation is unlike anything I've ever experienced. School, parties, women, they mean nothing. Cars, money, clothes, I couldn't care less. It's as if I've lost all desires and they've been replaced with the single, pinpoint idea, of understanding the lost moments of time from the other night's terror.

The way it strikes me, some kind of puzzle has been presented and my sole purpose is to solve that riddle. All else is a waste of time if it doesn't somehow help me to regain whatever has been lost. It's crazy, and I can't understand it, but it's the way I feel, and I can't seem to stop. Writing this journal makes the whole mess a little easier to understand. It kind of puts my thoughts in slow motion so I can take a concrete look at what's flashing through my head. They come so rapidly and seemingly from nowhere, like a clap of thunder rolling through clouds. Just writing, it really helps to sort through all the confusion.

Anyway, I'm going to keep writing. Hopefully I'll feel better soon, and this obsession will reveal itself as a temporary distraction, a mystery that resolves itself of its own momentum. I can't sit on the porch the rest of my life while my mind rakes over itself with questions and explanations.

One last thing, late in the day I received another piece of the pie. It only feeds the fires of my curiosity. People came in to visit. Maybe they were the last embers of delusion or hallucination finally burning out, but some seemed so familiar to me. That's what is such a mystery. One by one they showed up. I had nothing to say, so I listened. The familiar ones were nice, but my first visitors were on the scary side. Why would these people be coming to see me, and why were they talking to me?

Four

MEMORIES ONCE FORGOTTEN

School started. The university is packed with people waiting in lines, rushing to classrooms, or maybe just lying on the campus lawn, killing time between classes. The bookstore was wall-to-wall. The line wound all around the bottom floor, snaked up the stairs to the second floor and even through the rows of book stacks while people tried to squeeze by in search of whatever books, folders, and class outlines were on their list of required reading. That's not mentioning the hundreds of people pouring in and out of the cafeterias, the library, or the student center.

I got to campus around 8:30 and the parking lots were already full. Long lines must be some college rite of passage. The parking lot is no exception. I understand the drill now. Someone emerges from campus, the first car in line moves out and crawls behind the person to their car. Wait till they leave, pull in, and finally you're ready to begin the day. How long this system has been working I don't know, but everyone seems to follow the rules. There are a few stragglers though. They drive from parking lot to parking lot hoping to get lucky and find an empty space. It's a system based on miracles. That's usually me, but the percentages are much better to just wait the ten or fifteen minutes in line. Especially if you absolutely have to make it to class, like on a test day or something important. Just arrive early and wait in line.

About eight-forty I was at the front of the line and five minutes later I was out of my car and heading to my first class at nine. Life is still quiet even though sounds are everywhere. Strange. Thirty thousand people, thirty thousand college students, all congregating in the same general area, talking, yelling, laughing, and yet silence is everywhere, like an overtone or undertone or background color. My legs and arms are heavy, like they aren't my own? My mind is numb too. Life unfolds slowly and methodically. Normally I wouldn't have waited in line but it didn't matter. I pulled in line without a thought. I waited without a thought. I headed off to class without a thought.

The numbness was actually kind of nice. I think Pink Floyd captured the feeling without flaw in Comfortably Numb. There's brokenness and equal portions of peace at the same time, intertwined and blended together. I love songs like that. So many inspired artists have captured bits and pieces of emotion, carved and preserved with the talent of their craft. Many times I'll find myself spontaneously singing a song, and then I'll realize the song matches my mood almost perfectly. The musical library in my head must be filled with so many songs; in any instant, I can play a song tailored for that exact instant. I wonder if other people's minds work like that or not. Maybe it's because I love music so much. Music somehow manages to capture the emotion of life, much like poetry I guess. It's been soothing having a poetess in my head, always playing songs for the mood and moment.

Comfortably Numb was playing when I stepped out of my car and headed to class. I parked on the east side of school so I had to walk all the way across campus to get to Storm Hall. The campus road winding around the university in a giant, deformed circle wasn't too packed so I could have driven, but the only lot on the west side where I had an actual chance of parking is the Pit, and I hate walking up that steep long concrete stairway leading to the classrooms. Call me lazy, I decided to make the walk across campus.

I could have made it. It only takes maybe ten minutes to walk across campus and that would have left me with five minutes to spare. Somewhere along way, I ran out of steam. Maybe I was a bit too comfortably numb. I passed the bookstore and walked past the east side cafeteria and down the steps towards the library when I realized I wasn't going to go to class. It's hard to describe on paper; I just didn't care. I didn't care much about anything. I kept walking towards class for another hundred yards as I figured out school was not on the menu. Missing the first day wouldn't be the end of the world, but it's definitely a pretty crappy start for the semester. It's usually not until the spring when burnout sets in that I start missing classes.

By the way, I'm at the beach now. I've been here since one o'clock this afternoon. For some reason, watching people on campus really started to depress the social aspect of me. They seemed so connected and I felt so disconnected. To get away and be alone was all I wanted. I'm at the spot where I always surfed when I was young, Ollie's Peak. Remember, it's the one by Del Mar? Not over by the million dollar homes lining the beach, over towards the south where the cliffs start. I sat on an old concrete bench by the grass-covered hill where all the summer concerts are, and then I took the path, the one that leads down to the beach just before the cliffs start. The restaurant on the beach is still there, right on the sand. Even during the weekdays it's pretty crowded. The wood deck patio was totally full when I got here, people enjoying life.

It didn't take long sitting with the sea breeze blowing in my face and listening to shouts and laughter till depression really set in. It's like I'm in mourning. I've lost something? Maybe me.

I wandered on the sand along the base of the cliff for a while, dragging my feet through the sand, staring out into the clear sky and watching the surf. The waves are massive. A swell must have hit all of a sudden because it had been totally flat the day of the dream. There must have been a big storm offshore. Maybe it's still coming?

I walked for close to thirty minutes when a subtle prompting urged me to stop and look back at the cliffs. There it was, still there, the " Warning - Unstable Cliff " sign half way up the ledge. It's the sign that marks Ollie's Peak, right where we used to surf. It's been so long since I've been here. I was probably seventeen last time. Everything seems just the same. I guess the beach doesn't change too much. The seagulls are still here, the pelicans, the roar of the waves. I wish I could go back to those days. Life was so simple and pure. Now I've screwed everything up.

The sign brought back the nostalgia of those younger days. I remember the summer months, relaxing all day, surfing, sleeping, lying out in the sun, playing volleyball, and then surfing again. No work, no school, no worries. The memory has really sickened me. What's wrong with me? All the good times are lost, like they've been erased, and the future looks dim and uneventful. I wish I could go back and live in those days forever.

The Peak seemed like a good place to end my walk so here I sit, watching the waves and feeling really empty and sorry for myself. A funny thing did happen though. I'm still not sure if I believe it, or if I imagined it, but it fits in perfectly with the rest of the insanity. I don't know if it was an unsynchronized wave breaking an instant too soon, or a sudden shriek of a child passing by, but an impulse caused me to look up. In that moment I heard the voice. This time it wasn't inside my head. Someone was talking to me.

"It's a nice day out!"

The voice echoed through the air. It was hauntingly crisp and clear. Ollie! I sat there, facing the water, unable to open my mouth and confirm that it really was my old friend. He was riding by on a bicycle.

Ollie is someone I've known all my life. When I say that, I mean that in my first memories on this earth, he was there. He is as much a part of them as I was.

We all have close friends, but this was different. I don't mean a different type of friend. I mean he was different, always smiling and laughing. Not that we weren't, but he liked to dream, all fun and games. There was a bright side in everything and no one could convince him differently. And the way he went through life? Just skating along, shielded by a bubble of pure optimism. Maybe I'm becoming his complete opposite.

We'd been the closest of friends, then we drifted, not because we'd outgrown each other or anything like that. We just did different things, had totally different outlooks maybe. I honestly think he read one too many fairytales. That's where our roads went different ways.

Sometimes I close my eyes and try to remember what his last days were like, how his last hours were spent, whom he was with, and what they talked about. As best as I can remember, it went like this: He had taken his last final at about 4:00 on that Wednesday. I'm not sure exactly how long it took, but when he was finished, he walked with a friend up to her car. It's hard to remember her name right now.

Anyway, during the search, it turned out this girl was the last person to ever see Ollie before he disappeared. I see it before my eyes just like I was there. He'd waited after class for her to finish the test. He was usually pretty fast where tests were concerned, maybe because he was smart, and maybe because he didn't really care. He must have waited on the steps outside class for at least fifteen or twenty minutes. After what seemed like an eternity, the doors opened and there she was. They floated up the steps leading to the courtyard and headed off towards the street on the south side of campus. He'd parked his car on the other side of school, but it was getting dark, and he probably wanted to make sure she was safe.

The walk wasn't any faster than all the other nights they'd made the same walk, but this time I can strongly sense he wanted time to stop forever. You see, this was the end of the semester, the last day of class. Each time I see the image it is in slow motion, two little birds taking their last flight together. I can never speed the images up.

Once near her car, he would usually turn off to the left and head back to his car, but this night he didn't want to end so he asked her for a ride to his car. The picture looks like crystal. She is driving a white Jetta, they are talking, the radio is playing, and the sun has set. What are they talking about? I'm not sure. I think he's giving directions to his car while she's talking about the vacation she will be taking over Christmas. He must not be too sure where they are going because they end up doing circles around the parking structure until finally finding the parking lot where his car is. Maybe the detour was just to slow time?

From the moment they left class to the minute they arrived at his car, time stood still. Would it be their last time together? It couldn't have been more than fifteen minutes but clearly it was an eternity. This I know. These last few moments flash through my memory the most. It's been so long, but the moment I see them it's a nostalgic déjà vu. She is smiling as she says good-bye. Her smile is so very tender and sweet, almost as though somewhere deep inside she somehow knew of the future? She tells him that she'll call when she gets back from her trip with her boyfriend. He slowly gets out of her car and he's saying something too. I think it's "Goodbye". She never even got the chance to call.

It happened that very evening, the last day of the fall semester, the day of the test. At first no one knew what happened. He just disappeared. He didn't show up at home or school and no one heard from him.

What happened is still a mystery. Had he fallen asleep? It was as simple as that, he fell asleep and never woke, right there in his car. I sometimes get the feeling he died of a broken heart?

The funny thing is, in the middle of this hellish experience I'm living, Ollie of all people would come by and tell me what a great day it is? I'm in the middle of the most horrible experience I can imagine! Life sucks. It's just a waste with moments of joy sprinkled in every once in a while. If I didn't feel so empty I'd probably be crying for myself right now. How could life slip away like it has?

This journal is starting to sound real depressing. Maybe this is how it starts? I don't feel like living anymore. The emptiness is hurting real bad. I don't want to exist. I wish I were asleep so I didn't have to be conscious. How do suicide notes sound anyway? Are they filled with the same confusion and gloom that's in this journal? I better watch myself. I'm beginning to get a little scared of this depression. Why did I even bring this stupid journal with me? I should throw it away or burn it.

I guess it's all my fault. I don't know if I'm going to make it off this beach. If I summoned all my will, I might be able to stand up, but I don't think I have the inner strength to get up off my ass and make the journey all the way back home.

Five

EYE OF THE STORM

*I*t'll be sunset in a few hours. I'm not sure why, but I
don't want it to go down. I think it's the night, the darkness that gets me, the silence too. Last night was the final
blow; I can't fight anymore. Whatever storm was out there finally came ashore and crushed me.

If tonight holds more of the same, I doubt I'll be here tomorrow. It was grace I made it through last night. Maybe I'm
capturing the last days of my life? I remember the sun was
making its descent into the ocean, and rays of light were
bouncing off the approaching clouds, glowing and shimmering
on the waters. Far in the distance the sky filled with lightning.
A few people passed on the sand. The sound of waves, the
people, the sunset, the approaching clouds, and the lightning
illuminated sky must have lulled me into oblivion.

A bolt from nowhere hit with an unbelievable thud. Darkness had replaced the light and lightning erupted in quick flurries over the water. The storm had arrived. My eyes shuttered
as flashes of light burst into the sky. The combination trans-
ported the night sky into a living strobe.

"Prove your Faith!"

The thought didn't merely bubble to the surface, it exploded.

A few drops of rain fell, one on my arm, one on my neck, and one on my right leg. Rain began pouring from the heavens as a light, foggy mist swished and swirled. Visibility reduced to a matter of yards. My sheepskin jacket soaked, water from my hair dripped onto my T-shirt, and my legs went numb cold.

Hour by hour, the rain, the cold, and my lack of sleep wore on me. I perched myself on the wet, packed sand and looked over the sea. My body shivered and my clothes felt like a dank blanket soaked in water, draped around me like a cloak of muck. The water sucked up most of my body heat and when the wind blew the fresh air would cut into my skin like icicles. My breath was forced from my lungs in quick, erratic contractions, as my ribs clamped down upon my belly.

Prove your faith? Prove your faith? The time to solve the puzzle had come. No more waiting for tomorrow or some illusive treasure at the end of a rainbow that makes everything better, restoring all. I put my mind on the puzzle, poking here and there, bending, twisting, and wrestling with thoughts, possibilities, problems, and solutions. Layer by layer, I peeled off one cloak after another until I stood in sheer nakedness. It came down to whatever dwells in my own heart. Only God could save me.

At first, I thought I simply had to sit and endure until my Savior came for me, to save me from hell. When was he coming? How long would I have to wait? Would he come before I died here on the beach in this terrible storm? Maybe that's the way it works I thought. Maybe my destiny was to die on the beach in the middle of the storm and *then* the Savior would come?

"Go deeper into the waters!"

These occasional phantom thoughts emerging in my mind

are nothing new now. I decided to start listening. Prove my faith, I had to be perfect.

The dilemma presented itself: a demonstration of faith was called for. How great was my faith? Surely the Lord was watching me in my fight. Surely the Spirit of Love itself was with me?

"Walk out on the water! Prove your faith!"

Here came the test. Who was speaking? What was tempting? I returned to the scriptures yet into the water I went, right up to my knees. The winter ocean was frigid in the midnight hour as I tried to gain my balance in the current.

"Go Deeper into the Waters! Prove your faith!" was the command and up to my waist I marched, still deeper, further into the waters. The storm had created some monstrous waves, and although I'm a good swimmer, I had to fight just to keep standing.

"Go Deeper into the Waters! Deeper! Prove your faith!"

Doubt crept into my heart. At this depth I lingered, unable to command my muscles to move one step forward, or even an inch backward. More debate took place. I always found myself on the losing end. Whatever force gave life to my opponent, I could neither see through its deception nor out-reason its logic. I held on to what I still had. The Lord was my only hope. I walked further, up almost to my neck. Waves engulfed me, salt water washed into my mouth as I gasped for breath.

"Go Deeper into the Waters! Deeper!"

Death was now a serious possibility and maybe something deeper realized I was in terrible danger. Up until then, the threat to my life had not been immediate, but now, the insanity had become all too real. Who or what was this voice telling me to go deeper? Maybe it was the Tempter himself?

"He who finds his life will lose it, and he who loses his life for my sake will find it! Kill yourself to prove your faith!"

This thought was rabid in my head. I couldn't get it out as

it spread through every crevice and synapse of my brain. Over and over and over, I tried to solve the riddle. Did I want to live? Yes. But then I lose my life, where is my faith?

The question kept being presented, "But he who loses his life will find it . . ."

Up became down, left was right, and right was easily seen as wrong. The ensuing debate was all but impossible to win; after all, I was debating myself. My own intelligence had risen up against me. There was no way to mentally reach a conclusion in the state of mind I was in. The consequences were the ultimate, my life.

The more I debated, the more confused I got, and finally, death came. I was ready to die. I was ready to greet death with absolutely no resistance. There, in the freezing waters, my last ounce of energy burned. The candle dimmed, flickered a bit, and blew out with the wind. And then I heard myself speaking these magical words.

"My life is in the hands of Jesus Christ. I want only love, burn everything else. "

Over and over I spoke those words as I sucked down ocean water again and again. "Jesus will answer for me. Whatever is his will is my will. His will be done. I trust perfectly in him. Ask him the question. If he says die, then let me die."

I had repeated my solution nearly forty times when I heard some lunatic screaming out along the shore. He was jumping up and down, waving his arms, and pretty much dancing around like some kind of jumping bean. I caught a glimpse of him, he looked like a crazed beach bum, about as old as death itself. He kept yipping and yelling until I finally turned around.

When I got to shore, he was gone. He may never know it, but most likely he saved my life. I looked up. In the shadows of the night I saw the sign that marks Ollie's Peak. I curled into a little ball and prayed for the morning to come, for the sun.

All night long I listened to the waves washing up against the shoreline. Occasionally I'd get a glimpse of white water shining in the moonlight as it crashed and moved towards the beach. Why don't the sounds have any bite? It's just so quiet. It makes me feel so alone. I'm like a ghost in the midst of some strange world. I wish so much there was someone I could talk to. Something is terribly wrong? I'm in the midst of some thick, silent fog that has me trapped in its hypnotic grip.

Where's my family, my parents and sister? The haze has separated me. It's so quiet. My heart hurts so much I can't breathe. Maybe I'm dead already? I'm a ghost condemned to walk the earth in isolation and silence, imprisoned in a world filled with beauty and joy, only unable to take part. With each passing day I'll be less and less a part of this world, until people won't even be able to see me. I'll be sitting right here on the beach, right in front of them, and they'll look directly at me, right at me, and they won't know I'm here. Maybe some deeper part will realize they've just seen the ghost of a lost soul but they'll just look away and keep walking. I already feel it happening.

This is only my second day here and I'm already fading. Yesterday some people talked to me, but I must have started fading, because they seemed really confused and couldn't quite understand what I was telling them. After a while they started ignoring me and talked to each other as if I wasn't there, right in front of me! They were staring as if they couldn't quite see me anymore. After a while they left.

My clothes are a little damp still. I'm kind of cold, and I'm not sure if I can trust anyone. Some people seem to look right through me and others are staring for a while. Maybe the nice people can still see me, and the ones who might hurt me can't? Maybe the nice people can't see me, and the evil ones can?

I knew a nice lady once, she had such pretty blue eyes. If they have blue eyes, then I can trust them, otherwise I won't say anything. I'll just sit here and not say anything, and if they hurt me, then I'll have to let them, because maybe they don't know what they are doing. I'll be like Christ and turn the other cheek. If I follow the scriptures, then I'll be safe.

I wish so much I wasn't alone right now. I'm too frightened to move. I know God won't let anything bad happen to me.

My God, what have I done? What's wrong with me? Am I in hell? Did I kill myself last night? God, why did you let this happen to me? Don't you love me? I tried so hard to be beautiful in your eyes.

I remember how wonderful life was. Please, please let me go back. This can't be the way things are supposed to be. I remember when I was young, how happy and content I was. I was filled with your love in every moment, and I just couldn't stop smiling and laughing. Was that all a dream? Is this just a dream? Please be real, God; I can't go on without you anymore. Life is too empty and dark without your love. I can't seem to connect with the love in this world. It seems so fickle and self-serving. Remember how special I felt? I know you were there with me. You had to be. Why can't I remember?

All those fairy tales and poems and movies with happy endings, Santa Claus, and the Easter bunny - I've been living in a bubble of delusions my whole life. How could I have turned out to be anything but a dreamer? Why didn't I just look around and see all the suffering, all the heartache and the pain that others were enduring. Maybe then I'd have realized that hopes and dreams don't just magically happen. No wonder my world has fallen apart. I've built the whole damn thing upon illusion and some false inner voice that keeps telling me everything will work out perfectly. It tells me how wonderful and beautiful and special I am. It tells me my dreams are right around the corner. It tells me I can do anything. It tells me it loves me. Those are the things I've built my world on, one lie after another.

I wonder how long it takes until people stop believing? I've been the ultimate sucker. Even now I hold on to those words. It just shows you, if you hope for something bad enough, you'll believe just about anything. That's my problem; I want to believe those words so badly. My heart can't live in a world devoid of hope, hope at least for a beautiful ending.

For so long the voice has told me that this hurt is going away, but it seems to get worse and worse. It's like there's someone inside getting more and more lonely each day. The isolation is increasing. The air is getting thinner, and the darkness grows thicker every day I'm alive.

The voice keeps me going though. And now, if I force myself to look at the truth, the voice has been lying to me all my life, one promise after another. Each time I hear, I get so happy and excited, only to have the dream smashed to bits. Then, after hope is running out, I hear another lie and I'm filled with more false love and dreams. The whole process is killing me, bit by bit. How can I trust anyone? I can't even trust myself. Please help. God speed. Send an angel.

Six

THE SWEET SONG OF THE SUNSET

*L*ast night the sunset spoke to me. It was the sweetest whisper, such a beautiful sound. Its voice was so smooth and melodic. The smell of honey seemed to arise from the soft sand and meet the words at my ear. I've never imagined words can be so heavily soaked in love. They were honey soaked manna, food from the Gods. I could taste their essence as they filled me with emotions too intense to capture on paper. They told me about the ending. So pure and true, the words were like a flood of water pouring into my being and filling me with life, hope - true hope, a hope that meets in your chest, right in your heart, where it mixes with a faith that simply knows the truth. The ending is so beautiful. It washes away all the hurt, all the sadness. If I could only hold on to those words and never forget, I'd live in their sanctuary forever. How can anyone be really happy unless the sun has spoken to him? It seems like he'd be so alone.

All that starts to fade when you've heard the melody. There are such beautiful worlds that wait for us. So many heavens lie in our futures. There are so many reunions that wait. There are so many loved ones watching over us. They all wear the smile of compassion, a compassion that lives in the end and is filled with love. Angels dance and sing just out of reach and long for the day they'll hold us in their arms and reveal just how much they loved us as they nurture and urge us onward. So many glorious things are placed at our feet. So many memories are released and brought to light. Love is the truth; the rest is an illusion that served its purpose.

All those wrong turns weren't so wrong. The story was perfect. That's the truth. Sometimes only the ending can fix what we thought was failure. Dust turns to gold and water to wine. We are all so truly beautiful and courageous to have entered into this dream, a world of duality and self-created illusions. This is where true alchemy takes place.

I wish others could understand. I wish they could hear the ending. I wish they could feel the words, the love, and the beauty that patiently waits at the dawn. I've met so many kind and tender souls who are lost in this world. I wish I could tell them and show them the things I saw, the words I heard. These words hold an elixir of hope that melts through all sadness and isolation. So many people feel they've failed. So many hearts break when a loved one dies. So many people can't see their own beauty. Who is doing this to us? Why can't we see the light within ourselves? What convinces us we are anything less than what we are? I see it all around.

If only the sunset could be heard. For now it's my little secret. Some of the saddest stories have the happiest endings. If only those who struggle could hear. If only they would listen.

It wasn't until the middle of the sunset that I realized something was speaking to me. The music was always there. I just didn't realize it. And it *was* like music. I was sitting right here, at Ollie's Peak, when the sun started to set. It was as beautiful as ever. Soft, gentle blues painted themselves on the bellies of thin white clouds as the sun began to sink. A reddish glow mixed in the clouds and took on a light purple hue. The wind died and the ocean's surface became smooth as silk as it took on a glassy texture. The picture was simply too impressive to be real. Tears were dripping down my chin when I heard the voice.

"My beautiful child, listen to your heart, within it holds a most joyous secret. It is the story of a great adventure that leads through countless worlds filled with treasures too great to be numbered. Some are gold and others merely the rust of illusion. It is an epic filled with glory and sorrow, a story overflowing with victory and defeat. It is a tale of love and hate, tragedy and triumph, life and death, riches and poverty, uncertainty and destiny. It is a story of destiny. The pages are filled with words like hope and faith, peace and trust. Each stroke of the pen has been brushed on with complete and perfect love.

"With each page you move closer to the greatest of all loves. With each chapter you travel within a journey that began so very long ago. Try to remember, my child. Close your eyes and find the silence. Dip into the pools of creativity, where imagination and fantasy swim and play. These are the keys, beautiful one; they free you from the limitations placed upon your shoulders. Learn to listen to the music and soon enough the door will open.

"Remember where it began? The memory is still weak, sleeping in wait for the spring. Let the sunshine filter down through your body, and allow it to enter and nurture the seeds. The flowers will come. Relax and simply enjoy the moment. Give the memory time and imagine a beautiful city surrounded by lush green gardens filled with flowers from every color of the rainbow. Remember the beginning, and then you will have found your destiny. You will have found the end.

"Your light shined so bright in the early years. What was that like? Why was life so smooth and graceful? There were hard times. There were heartaches. Why didn't their seeds grow? You continued to glow with laughter wherever life brought you. I recall the presence of an unshakeable faith and trust. Was that because you remembered?

"It seems like ages, thousands and thousands of years ago that you smiled so brightly. The highs and lows have a way of breaking one. But that's really not what did it, is it? It's just that somewhere along the way you forgot. You fell asleep and lay there waiting for someone to come along with a magic dust that would heal all your wounds. I have that dust. You have always had that dust. It is all right there in the story. You've missed it because it lies between the lines. You've come so close so many times, yet you always turn the other way. You close your eyes and forget in your hands is a perfect story. A story you have created and written yourself.

"So many times you've returned to your slumber. It has a way of breaking one. Couldn't you hear the screams, the joyous shouts to wake up? Life is a gift. Life is a crazy ride that allows us to descend into illusion and experience emotions from a spectrum of unlimited possibilities. It allows us to live our dreams. You were able to see entire stories from beginning to end. You knew the lows would pass and the pain would fade. You were there for the endings. You saw faith and love return in an instant. You saw souls who thought they were worthless find out they were some of the most loved and respected spirits in all the heavens.

"And you saw the tears of men and women in the middle of the story. You saw them in the agony of the dream. You saw their hearts break, and you wanted to fill them with your love and light their candle with hope. You wanted them to see how magnificent their stories were. You wanted them to remember the ending. 'Inspiration' is one of your magic sounds. Now do you remember? Try to feel it.

"Can you laugh with me? Isn't it wonderful and amazing? You're right in the middle, right in the middle! Don't you see, you're right where you want to be. Wake up and remember. My love, you are so much stronger than you know. This is nothing for you."

For some reason, the spark in me returned. It's a simple matter of grace. Amazing Grace! Love brought me back, the constant and gentle song I used to hear every day at the sunset as a child. It was as if I'd been wandering in a non-existent daze, and ever so slowly, rays of light melted and thawed my soul until the breath of life returned. A very subtle energy started to build, and suddenly I was consciously present again. In that moment, the sunset was at its most magnificent.

Sometimes in my dreams, I've been surrounded by unparalleled beauty and overwhelming colors, but there can't be any birth as glorious as the creation of that second. There is no picture that can capture that moment.

I realized the lights and colors could be felt. Not only could they be felt; they could be heard. They were very clearly communicating. The sunset was speaking to me! The words came from all around, yet somehow, they emerged from deep inside. It was a voice from within, a voice from an inner beauty and tranquility, the voice of a Divine Mother. The words were music and the colors were emotion, and the lights were sound. How I'll ever capture the message on paper is beyond me? If I can paint a single speck, then possibly I've done more than I could hope for.

The last rays of the sunset were glistening on the ocean's silky surface as the sun's love washed through me in wave after wave of soothing, healing words. The voice flowed on.

"Sweetheart, smile, laugh and sing. All I tell you is your

destiny. The love that awaits you is real! Listen with all your heart and fill your ears with glee! I'm speaking to you about the kingdom, about the heavens, about Camelot! Imagine the architecture. See the flowing hills and flowers covering the meadows. Look to the mountains, capped with the whitest snow and blanketed with huge green pines. Call out to the butterfly and scream to the eagles! Flow down the rivers with fish and let them wash you into the City where the Angels work their miracles of light! Fall on your knees and thank the heavens for such beauty and love all living in perfect harmony!

Remember, my child, remember. You carry the key and the city within. You only have to remember. You only have to ask. Let go of all your suffering, little one. Let go of all your hurt, of all your fear. Once you have seen the city, how could anything possibly hurt you?"

Seven

NATURE SPIRITS

I feel so much better today. The haze wrapped around my mind seems to have vanished, just like the fog this morning. I woke up early, not long after the sun had risen. The roar of the waves crashed in the distance, pounding into the sand and shoreline. The low rumble has a bit of a soothing quality.

The whole beach was blanketed in a crisp, white, misty fog. It's very different from the haze that has been tormenting and confusing me. That haze is heavy and gloomy. It's dark and unfriendly. This morning, the fog had a light and airy feeling. It's a near perfect and cloudless day.

Just above the fog, the sun's rays must have been shining down with all their early morning warmth. The light from above bounced through the tiny water droplets of mist and lit up the air like a glowing snowstorm. The fog was thick and I couldn't see the waves or the shoreline, but somehow, the backdrop above, below, and in the distance, was illuminated in white light.

I've been sleeping under the bridge down at the river mouth. Most people would probably think it's horrible, but actually, it's kind of cozy. The bridge is wide, made of concrete, and goes right into the sand, kind of like a freeway overpass. I always loved it when I was young. The tide would come in and form a river that rushed in from the surf, under the bridge, and into the lagoon on the other side. We'd go into the surf and then ride our boogie boards into shore, funnel into the river, and ride the small rapids to the bridge.

It's a bit nostalgic or ironic, but I also remember one time when we were playing down at the river mouth. I couldn't have been more than six. After riding a wave down the river, a bit too far, and under the bridge, I saw a man sleeping on the concrete pillars that horizontally connect the bridge's legs for support. They're about three feet thick and run along the beach like a wall. They section off one part of the bridge from another. It's like the legs of the bridge are solid concrete walls that run the entire width of the bridge.

The thing is, in a few spots, maybe about six feet off the ground, there are nice, flat, wide ledges that are open all the way up to the bottom of the bridge. I remember that guy so well. I was a bit scared, and I just didn't understand what he was doing there. I think I wondered where his family was or what must have happened to him? He was lying on top of the piling, wearing some old faded jeans all frazzled on the bottom, no shoes, and a red and black checkered plaid shirt. Over that he had on some gray, wool jacket that was wrapped around him. He was asleep and never noticed me, but I thought he seemed so alone.

I guess I was feeling the sympathy and compassion a six-year- old is capable of. For a second or two, a deeper part of me connected and completely understood the depth of the isolation and loneliness this man was experiencing. I know I stopped walking and stared at him for a moment. Even though he was sleeping, in that instant, he wasn't alone.

Right now, it feels as if I was looking at an eerie glimpse of the future. The image of that little boy looking up and seeing

the bum sleeping on the exact same spot as I am now is a
haunting picture. At the time, the beautiful little boy had no
way of knowing, but now the dots have been connected. The
loop has been completed. I wonder if the young kid somehow
knew?

So here I am. Not only have I been sleeping under the
bridge; I seem to be trapped in that one moment I'd experienced as a child. What was then merely a blink or two of an
eye has become an inescapable eternity. I'm now living in that
moment. But the moment doesn't remain the same. It is
changing, and for that reason, I have hope. I believe so much
in the sunset. I know good things are possible. I know wonderful experiences await me. In all truth, things aren't so bad.
My little corner under the bridge really is kind of cozy. There's
a nice sandy walkway leading in from the rest of the beach, and
in between the pylon where I sleep and the next pylon, there's
a lagoon. Not a bad picture to wake up to every morning.

I don't have a cover but no wind gets under the bridge.
I've got some stuff that folds up and makes a pretty good pil-
low. Around ten at night there aren't quite so many cars going
by and by twelve it gets pretty quiet. Not to mention the beach
is one of the most soothing and healing places to be. If ever
I'm sick, this is where I'd wish to be.

The nights haven't been pleasant but the days can be really
quite nice, especially this morning. After I woke up, I had a
great time wandering in the fog. The simple act of walking
along the beach actually became a spiritual act!

When I started, it was real early and there were only a few
surfers getting ready to paddle out. The visibility was horrible
and I couldn't see the line-up out in the surf. I walked along
the shore, right at the water's edge, and the fog was so thick I
couldn't even see the houses lining the shore or the cliffs a little further down.

When the sun had climbed high enough, the lights danced

with the fog. Brilliant light was coming from above and water particles in the air everywhere caught a spark of light. An electrical current flowed through the air. The mist was the conductor and the energy massaged my soul, like taking a shower in light. I felt dirt and muck washing away.

My energy increased, and I walked faster and faster. The stream became a wind that blew right through me as if my body had no form. I wasn't quite sure where I was anymore. With a surge, the wind picked up and memories began to appear.

I was high on a mountain. Angelic crystals of light bounced through the air as tiny snowflakes whirled around with the wind. Cold mountain air was sharp and crisp as the wind grew and tiny ice crystals bit into my face. I couldn't see or understand where I was, but no questions or doubt arose. My eyes blinked furiously as sticky snow accumulated on my face. The ice felt like a cold heat digging deeper and deeper into my cheekbones and forehead. The rest of my body was surprisingly warm. Well, not warm, but I felt somehow insulated from the outside chill. The cold wasn't making its way down below my skin.

The wind swirled around me like an angry tornado that sought to transport me into another world. I could see no more than a foot or two in front of me, and as I looked down, I saw I was buried in snow, almost up to my knees. A delirious glee bubbled from within. A surge of inner laughter took me back to the age of three. It had been my first time in the mountains. Actually, the first time I'd ever seen snow at all. I can't remember what I was thinking or if I was even thinking at all. The beauty of the moment was that I simply *was* there. We had taken the gondola up near the summit and I had plopped down in the snow like it was a miraculous sand pit. Shear and total bliss was what I was feeling. Nothing has ever felt so free and pure. Scooping up snow, I poured it over myself as if I were bathing in God's love.

Lost in the experience, at first I didn't realize the snow had subsided to more of a light, spring flurry. All around, the ground was covered in a fresh and flaky sugar powder. The snow looked so fragile and fluffy. I wanted to dive into it like a mountain lake and swim deep in its belly.

Why does the mere presence of snow induce such a glee and uncontainable joy in kids? I was just barely able to contain myself enough to ease into the snow and look around. I was high on a slope just above a meadow of some kind. Beautiful and majestic pines lined the hillside, all covered and dripping with the fresh white powder that had just rained upon them. A few snowflakes were floating to the ground as the sights emerged from the snowy haze, until I had a wonderfully lucid picture in front of me.

How can I describe the feeling and sensations of a three-year-old little boy? I think what I felt was an awe, completely devoid of any humility, but without the slightest hint of ego. That's the most amazing part of the memory. I felt so utterly connected to everything! The green trees, the rolling hills, the valleys, and especially the snow, they all felt like part of me, even the white sky above, with the hazy clouds blowing by and shades of blue occasionally peeking through, filtering rays of sunlight onto the crystalline white snow. There didn't seem to be a sense of "I" within the picture. I didn't understand or grasp that the snow was not me, or that the trees were not me, or that the sky was not me. I was everywhere! At the least, I had no sense of boundaries. Where I stopped and other things began was so mild and delicate, it left me with a feeling of perfect freedom and unlimited existence. My glee was the perfect experience of feeling what I thought was my own beauty. The connection to the beauty around me was so intense and pure, I felt as if I *was* beauty itself! I was the tree. I was the snow. I was the sky. I was because I simply didn't realize I wasn't.

Those imprints still hadn't found root within my psyche.

I wonder how long the mind has to remain still for us to be able to escape briefly into different worlds or memories of the past? The whole time I was playing in the snow and feeling its healing, not once did my mind rise up and protest.

By myself I've never been able to quiet my mind, but lately, I've been slipping in and out of so many different places and times. It feels as though a Master of some degree is demonstrating his magic. He seems to come to me in one form or another. Sometimes it's the fog, and other times the sunset, or maybe even the sound of the ocean or the cry of a seagull. Whatever the disguise, this force seems to quietly brush up to me and engage my conscious mind. Almost effortlessly really, my thoughts seem to become lost in conversation.

Each time I'll wake later to find I'd been led astray, or at least part of my mind was. It's like some sleight-of-hand trick. My mind is always so noisy and constantly thinking, but this Master seems to understand its nature. One minute he is softly speaking and the next my mind has been diverted by some utterly meaningless and repetitive task. I kind of picture a hypnotist swinging his watch back and forth. My head is turning side-to-side, following the watch, and soon enough, my mind is mesmerized, completely lost and looking about as dumb as a rock! At that point, the Master kind of moves his hand over to the right, always careful to keep swinging the watch, and he says, "Ok, precious one, now that we've got him out of the way we can talk. I've got some wonderful things to share with you, so many lovely things to experience."

Now that I think about it, the hypnotist really isn't a fair way to describe the Master. Really, it's so far beneath him. Maybe long, long ago that would have been a good picture. The master is more of a beautiful siren. She is the most beautiful of creatures. All that's needed is a smile and an instant of eye contact and hours or even days later my mind wakes up, lying off in a field somewhere babbling to itself and not knowing what the hell happened. During that time, a deeper self will be off skiing the Alps or soaring through the heavens upon the wings of an eagle.

I've never really thought of it this way but maybe I am losing my mind, consciously! I seem to be ditching it at every possible opportunity. But then again, maybe the hypnotist is really a piper of some kind, trying to lead me astray and break my sanity? Maybe I need to fight and make sure these sleight-of-hand tricks don't get the best of me. I have to defend my mind. Now is the time to think and figure this thing out!

You know what? I'm not getting sucked back into this paranoia debate. I feel too refreshed and light right now to turn around and deal with myself. I'm too tired anyway. Who cares what I think? I know how I felt. I felt wonderful and free and alive again! That's what matters, isn't it? I've got to stop second-guessing every little thought I have. I wish I could silence the noise. I wish I could slip away again, back to the mountain where life was so bright and hopeful. It was such peace.

Where are those swirling snow flurries that so kindly swept me away? I'd been playing in the snow and marveling at God's beauty when they returned. I even saw my parents and sister, standing just a few yards from me. I loved seeing them so much but they all seemed a bit distant and sad, even my sister, who was only five at the time. They were watching me, wearing sad but sweet, compassionate smiles on their faces. The wind remained calm, but high above, the clouds gathered and meshed together, erasing any evidence of the sun. The air grew a bit cooler with the fading of the sun, and soon large, fluffy flakes of snow were floating down from the heavens. Slowly the green pines vanished from sight as the snow fell with more and more intensity. My family disappeared, taking their memory from me as if they never really were there. A fog filtered its way into the air, erasing the last few yards of sight.

Once again, I was lost in a white cloud of gleaming white crystals. The ice cold penetrated deep now and seemed to be purifying every tiny cell of life within. My foothold on the memory that only minutes earlier seemed so concrete and lucid drained from me. My last roots broke free, and then I was floating, upward and closer to complete oblivion in the ice crystals.

In that moment, the winds calmed to less than a whisper and the clouds descended upon me, into my soul, agreeing to aid in the illusion. I found I was captured in a bubble of pure white energy that had no dimensions, no limits, and nothing but smiling bliss. White out. I was weightless. Floating? Falling?

Nature caught me in the right moment, with just the right balance of light and white. In the instant that I could no longer see what was right in front of me, I realized I could see forever! Heaven first reveals itself in moments. Briefly, the veil parts and magically we are swept away.

Wave after wave of energy crested and broke over me. Bubbles of joy released from the bottom of my spine and raced towards the heavens. Laughter filled my ears. It was my own. Angels were singing their songs and lights were flashing in harmony. The electrical current and the blood flowing through my body became a liquid morphine seeping through every nook, cranny, and crevice of my being. I was singing! I twirled around and around and around with my arms spread wide open, flying free in the wind. I was the eagle, soaring through the heavens in a crazed barrel roll of delirium! I twirled faster and faster, sending my senses and perception into oblivion. I clearly heard the song "Circles in the Sand" playing over and over with such a rich tone. I felt the beauty of the music. "Never ending love is what we've found!"

I woke up on the warm beach sand. Or I should say, when I returned I was still gently spinning around in a circle, arms outstretched with more than a few people watching me in delight. While I'd been lost in an imaginary dream world, my actual physical body had most certainly been doing more than a few crazy things. By the look on their faces, I'd put on quite a show. At least they all had smiles. Maybe to them I'd been some eccentric nut or just a wild, free-spirited kid, playing and dancing with the dolphins and ocean breeze?

I'm glad there weren't too many people around though. Of course, I can't remember most of my walk. It must have been four or five miles long since I ended up below the cliffs down at Black's Beach. That's why not too many people were around. To get to the sand, you've got to take a pretty good hike down a steep but paved path that leads down through the cliffs to the beach. You have to drive into this neighborhood filled with palatial homes that overlook the water. The trail down from the glider port is a pretty tough hike too. That leaves only two other ways to get there, one of which is to swim in from a boat, and the other, well, I'm really the only one dumb enough to walk in along the beach from Del Mar.

I'm sure there were people on the beach in Del Mar, but really, it was pretty early in the morning when I'd left there. I doubt if too many people were watching me.

I don't care much about the people at Black's laughing at me. They were just a handful of surfers who ultimately probably forgot about me the minute they hit the water. I feel so shiny and clean anyway. I can't think of anything that would have bothered me. The sky had cleared to reveal a perfect, sunny day. The ocean water was a light, turquoise blue, which is unusual, but the water at Black's can get crystal clear sometimes. There wasn't a hint of wind, which made the ocean's surface a floating mirror of glass.

I plopped down in the sand and watched the waves in complete serenity for the rest of the day. What a peaceful place Black's Beach can be! The cliffs are so high and deep they block out nearly all noise from civilization, and the huge waves pounding on the shoreline created an easy melody that dribbled into my ears over and over.

This is the best I've felt in so long. Last week seems like eons of time ago. Whatever force had a hold on me, it's completely vanished. Like the sun's rays that slowly burned their way into the fog all morning until the watery mist in the air was dried into non-existence, leaving only a crisp, clear, sunny day, the loving energy that pulsed through my veins saturated and then overpowered the haze around my mind until only a lucid peace remained.

Today has been such a great day. I want every day to be like this one. Forever! Sitting on the warm, white sand, and watching the surfers and the waves all alone made me want to become some sort of invisible nature spirit that dances and plays in the soft sand and cool waters, slipping in and out of worlds. I kept imagining I was one of these creatures, invisible to everyone around.

You know, I really think it was working. Life went on all around me as if my existence had no effect at all. The surfers rode their waves; some joggers occasionally ran by, a plane flew over, brushing the water. Seagulls were flying around looking for food and little sand pipers ran along the shore as the waves retreated, trying to get a nibble of a sand crab or shrimp. Farther out pelicans dove into the water and scooped up some fish to fill their bellies. I even saw three schools of dolphins playing and riding the waves. Life hadn't changed one bit. The world would go on perfectly without me. It's almost a little scary just how insignificant losing me would be. Who would know? Not the surfers in the water and certainly not the seagulls or the pelicans. Not even the dolphins would realize my disappearance, or that I ever existed at all anyway.

That left me a little lonely, but still, I made every effort to conceal myself and become a nature spirit. I was truly a ghost.

Sure a few people saw me, but the minute they turned their heads in the other direction, I disappeared from their thoughts. The effect is just about the same as if they'd never known my existence anyway. It makes me kind of wonder how many times I've seen or felt the presence of some type of spirit and it just didn't register in my consciousness. How many times have I done this? I experienced it first-hand today. All the people on the beach who crossed my path, even though they were looking right at me, most never saw me, and even the others who had enough focus to see me, forgot within less than an instant. It was done so quickly, I'm sure their minds were never able to register and store the memory. Except for one strange bird. In fact, I'm pretty sure it was the same beach bum who was yelling at me the other night. For all I know, he might have been staring down at me for well over an hour. I was facing the water, so naturally I couldn't have seen him high on the cliffs behind me. His stare and intent were so powerful. That was my first recognition of him. I felt someone or some force on my shoulder, watching me. I turned around and looked up, sure enough, there he was. I couldn't make him out in too great detail. If it's possible from such a distance, I made eye contact and we locked our gaze in a firm acknowledgement of each other's presence. I wanted to yell, "I see you too!"

Instead, I tried with all my might to disappear and erase my memory, the way I'd done so easily with the others. This guy never wavered, though. We locked in our gaze for a very long minute or so and then I looked away. I turned around and watched a perfect twelve-foot wave crest and throw itself down into the ocean. I looked out towards the water and searched for the dolphins. It was my way of saying "So what. I don't care what you want or think. I've already forgotten you."

That old bag stayed up there the whole day watching over me. Every single move and with every breath, I felt his presence on my shoulders. I never managed to muster up the courage to look back over my shoulder and see if he was still there. I knew he was. I know he was.

Towards the end of the day, when I got up to leave, he was still up there with his hawk eyes fixated on me. I didn't give him the satisfaction of looking back, nor did I say goodbye. He was there. I felt his presence. I looked at the sand and started the long trek back to Del Mar.

The whole walk I kept wondering about him. I know he meant no harm or anything like that. He just seemed to be saying, "I see you". It was his way, but it doesn't make much sense.

Oh well, it's just about sunset now and without doubt, that's my favorite time. I like to settle in here at Ollie's Peak and watch the waves and the birds as the sun starts to descend from the heavens and eventually merge with the ocean and sink down into tomorrow. I feel so peaceful now that the poison is out of my system. I'm not sure I could have endured another day or even an instant in that gloomy haze.

What beautiful power love contains! I feel as though I'm perfectly content with the moment. I could live in this moment forever! In fact, that is my plan. Possibly I've found my destiny. The peace and love in this lovely place are immeasurable. Soothing solitude seems to be just about everywhere.

The sun's rays have formed a glistening road on the water that leads right to me while I write these words. Who said magic doesn't live! The path leads right to me, right where I'm sitting! Or is it the road laid before me? Either way, *here* is exactly where I'm supposed to be. What a comforting thought. It takes all the worry and second-guessing away. Everything is perfect. Divinely and gracefully perfect. There have been no mistakes. There is only the perfect place to be and the perfect moment to be there. This is where I now live, at the end of the rainbow. Or is this the foot of the rainbow? What's on the other side? No matter, the light is clearly shining to this spot, right at Ollie's Peak. No wonder he loved it here!

Eight

IRON ASS

I 'm afraid I lost sight of the goal. Between the sweet song of the sunset and the peaceful bliss of yesterday, I forgot about the quest, this mystery that has to be unveiled, the pieces of my life that have to be put back together. It's the reason I'm here at the beach anyway. Nothing else mattered.

If the flame smoldered over the last couple of days, today the fuse was relit with all intensity. I have to discover the meaning. I must find the key to this strange world I'm in! I have to stay focused and make sure I don't become diverted again, or lulled into a lackadaisical aloofness that convinces me nothing is wrong.

Today reaffirms the existence of some sort of divine puzzle I'm living in. I met the beach bum, Iron Ass. His name illustrated his insanity right from the get go, but I had no idea. He talks like a complete lunatic, always pausing in the middle of a speech or thought to cackle like a hyena or some crazed dog. And the way he talks! It's like he's running at light speed. One minute he'll be talking about one subject and in the next he'll be a mile down the road on some tangent about vegetables being very healthy.

I wasn't even close to prepared for a nut like this guy to

walk over and say hello. "Hello Oliver, I am Iran Ass, the Lone One! I'm here so you can figure things out. I'll show you what you know." He winked at me and then said I could have the privilege of simply calling him Iron Ass. There was plenty of laughter in my head; no doubt more than a few have gotten the same greeting.

Those first few seconds, I figured he was merely a funny old man who liked to tell stories. Old and a bit senile? Probably. A guide? Absolutely not.

He was wearing a light tan corduroy type of pants with a thin, black belt that held the pants firmly to his waist. A tall, thin man with an unkempt beard, mostly gray with white mixed in, he had on a bright, almost fluorescent Hawaiian colored shirt, and over that he had a black leather vest he left unbuttoned. His shoes were some type of leather moccasins, and they were tan like his pants. On his head he wore an Indiana Jones type of hat with a deep, dark purple feather sticking out the back. Also, he had on some type of Indian necklace or trinket. It was on a thin leather rope around his neck and on it hung a sapphire blue amulet made of ivory. It hung just over his heart between the breastplates. With all the colors, it's amazing it stuck out so much.

I found myself smiling. This guy was really funny. Harmless and definitely funny. He walked up slowly. Once he opened his mouth, however, it was like he'd plugged himself into the light switch. He babbled at an amazing speed about the sun and the moon and how the weather was absolutely perfect. He somehow made his way to the subject of his shoes and from there he started ridiculing *me* about the way I was dressed. He was hilarious. Honestly, he missed his calling; he should have been a stand-up comedian.

"First of all, how do you know my name?" I asked, "and second of all, if anyone or anything is going to help me figure out what the hell is going on, it's not going to be you. That's for sure."

"Of course I know your name," said Iron Ass, "In fact, I know everything that you know and you know everything I know only you just haven't realized it yet! Everything is a reflection of either your knowledge or your creativity. Any book you read, any person you talk to, they are merely reflecting what you already know or what you have created. One day, you'll see just how creative and just how much knowledge you have. There isn't anything here you don't already know."

Lucky me I thought, homeless, living on the beach, and now I've got a crazed beach bum who calls himself Iron Ass telling me he's going to help.

He spoke as if he'd read my thoughts. "And you think I'm funny? Ha! You're the crazy one, and here you are calling me nuts!"

"Look," I said, "I think it's pretty clear who the crazy one is here."

The old guy responded with surprisingly quick wit, "To those who sleep, the awakened ones appear to dream, and to the insane, even the truth appears as a lie born of insanity!"

"Well, Buddha," I laughed, "Now you're saying something that at least sounds wise."

Iron Ass began to sound a little sincere. "Look Oliver, at best I am a reflection. You look at me and see insanity because you're looking in the mirror. Yes sir! Even so, I've got the cure, and I've got to give it to you! So I'm giving it to you so you can get it, so you can receive it. Get it! Got it! If I gave it to you straight, you'd never grasp it anyway."

"Okay, now you're confusing me, Iron Ass."

He always responds so quickly. "If you talk to a duck, you quack, and if you want to say hello to a dog, you bark!"

"Please, Iron Ass!" I said, "Try to focus a bit for me. How does all this relate to me? What does it have to do with my having these hallucinations and coming down to the beach to try and quench this burning desire to understand?"

"Oliver, we need the basic elements of the puzzle laid out for us. We need to understand the nature of the dream! That's all."

"The nature of what dream?" I asked.

"The nature of the dream is that it lies all around us. It's everywhere and in everything. It's part of you, it's part of me, it's part of us all! Hell, everything you see, feel, touch or smell is just part of the dream. It's an experience created by the mind and held together so firmly that it appears to be solid. That's the illusion folks! That's just what they want you to believe, isn't it! Ha! To me it's just some fancy brushwork mixed in with just enough common sense to keep us all believing."

I still can't believe the conversation I was having. "Iron Ass, I must really be desperate because you almost sound like you know what you're talking about. All I know is I'm more confused than ever and there is something extremely important for me to figure out."

Those first few words were all it took, they uncorked my entire story and I sat with Iron Ass for hours, telling him every last detail. I told him about the dream, and the ritual, and quitting school to come and live at the beach.

After listening, he finally spoke, "So the seed has been planted. You'll find what you are searching for. The answers are all around you, and you already know-um. Look at life then; look at the dream, and try to understand what is. Focus on that, and the answers will come. The nature of the dream will unfold before you like a magical song. Yeah! Now you're getting closer! Listen some more then. The nature of the dream is that intent is everything. You'll see what you want to see and hear what you want to here. This is what I'm saying 'your perception will be the filter through which you interpret the dream.'

"You already got the pieces, otherwise you wouldn't be here

in the first place. What you've got to do is sit down and put the pieces together, make-um fit and see what you're holding on to. It's all within you. Trust me on that one."

Old Iron Ass had me hooked. "How do you know all this stuff?" I asked him.

"Because I've been through the experience."

"Iron Ass," I said, "I can kind of follow what you're saying, but that doesn't explain all the weird feelings and the strange ideas that keep popping into my head. It's like I can't think straight, and eventually I just get worn out and depressed."

Iron Ass always answers so quickly and without any pre-thought, it really gives him an air of confidence. "Simple, it's the crap coming out."

That time I understood him. "You mean it's all the things my mind is digging up, but if that's the case, why have some been beautiful and loving thoughts and feelings?"

"When you dig into the dirt, sometimes you find a treasure. Keep the treasures and get rid of the crap." Iron Ass finally was making some sense.

"But thoughts and ideas come so fast I can't see through them. Sometimes I can't tell what is crap and what isn't."

Iron Ass started to answer my question even before I asked it. "Treasures are very subtle, speak softly, and come from love. Crap screams at you and is not gentle. The crap in your head is speaking to you."

Now Iron Ass was getting away from me a bit. "What does that mean, it speaks to me?"

"It speaks to you and you like to listen to it."

I think Iron Ass was taking the offensive, trying to confuse me or something, but I tried to keep following him. "You're telling me that all the things in my head, all my thoughts, they speak to me somehow?"

"You'll see," he said, "You might even meet the monster face to face before this is over!" He was laughing while he said that, so it must have been a joke.

I left right after and sure as Iron Ass had said, the wheels in my mind are spinning harder than ever. I keep going over and over what he said. The fire to solve this puzzle is all I can think of. The more time goes by, the more intriguing this mystery becomes. Iron Ass's life alone is enough to keep me thinking for the next few days.

In 1960 Iron Ass had been a bit of a flower child. His whole family, which was a large one, had been swept away by the times and they were the stereotypical hippies. Sixty-five was the year that Iron Ass met Amy. She was five years younger at twenty-nine. The attraction was undeniable and they married before the year's end. Amy was a thin blonde with a smile that Iron Ass says could melt any heart.

For four years they traveled the country, stopping briefly in just about every major city along the way. After their travels ran out of steam they ended up in a suburb outside of Los Angeles. There, Iron Ass found his first real full time job. For whatever reason, business came easy and within five years he had become an extremely successful businessman. Compared to the life he had been living, it was night and day. His time was filled with charity benefits and concerts and trips down to the beach. With Amy at his side, Iron Ass said it was the closest to heaven he had ever been. He was hopelessly lost in love and everything he had in the world, he had accomplished simply because he loved her so much. Business came effortlessly even though he spent a great deal of time and energy pursuing his dreams.

Sometimes things seem too good to be true, and it took only one blow to send his life into a tailspin. At the age of thirty-nine, beautiful Amy started to feel tired and rundown almost all the time. The nightly walks along the beach ended, and so did the dining and dancing, the plays and the opera. Most of her day was spent in bed sleeping. The doctors diagnosed

Amy with a rare form of leukemia and she died before the age of forty.

Nine long and painful months passed before Amy lost her fight. Iron Ass quit his job and spent every moment by her side. Seeing her suffer so long and slowly was too much for him. He wished that if only he could take her place, then life wouldn't be so cruel. Until the troubles in the world came so close, he had never accepted them as real.

Life lost meaning and pain turned to hate. He had been betrayed by God himself! God had always been in his heart and he never questioned that love for a second. His faith had been unshakeable. But how could God have taken away the one thing he loved so dearly? It was the only thing in the world he really cared about, his only desire. The money, the cars, and the house, were just things that had come to him, he never asked for or felt a need for them. His only need was Amy and she was slowly pried from his arms.

After Amy's death, all Iron Ass sought was solitude. Maybe one day he could find peace, but he would never be the same. Some tragedies cut too deep. Would trust ever return?

In his search for solitude, Iron Ass found himself living at the beach, sometimes weeks at a time. As a homeless man, the beach was quiet and lonely, and it gave him a place to escape. He carried Amy in his heart and by the stillness of the ocean, he felt very close to her. He felt her spirit. With every ounce of his being, he wished that he too wasn't a part of the world anymore. His only desire had been extinguished, and life was empty.

For years Iron Ass's life became darker and darker. He searched and searched for happiness and peace but all he found was sadness and depression. He held on to Amy the whole time and thought death was his only answer. Each day, he did the same things and had the same thoughts. The monotony of life caused him to sink even deeper into the darkness.

On his last trip, Iron Ass decided he would never again leave the beach. The agony had become too great, and in its most intense moment, a spark was lit. The flame smoldered, flickered, and then stabilized. He was going to change his life. His ego had somehow taken hold, and he had been caught in misery. The answer he came up with was *denial.* He would simply deny his ego. He started to apply the laws of opposites. If an archer keeps missing his target to the left, then it's best to aim to the right.

He didn't wear his nice clothes, he didn't cut his hair, and he sold all his belongings. He completely turned his world upside down. If society said one thing, he thought another. If he was supposed to act one way, he acted the other. Red was green and up was down.

In retrospect, Iron Ass says that complete denial of the self is a surefire way to insanity. Apparently it's pretty quick too. After two months of living in solitary and thinking the opposite of every thought that came into his head, Iron Ass became more and more confused. An actual voice started speaking in his head. If he decided he was hungry, the other voice would say he wasn't hungry. If he thought he was tired, the other voice would say he was wide awake. First he would lie down, and then a minute later he would get up. Iron Ass became a complete lunatic; unaware of who he was, as all his thoughts were canceling each other.

In this crazed state, Iron Ass says, he entered into the middle worlds. Whether it's a miracle or simply the grace of God I don't know, but Iron Ass wound up at the doors of a Zen Temple.

When he arrived, the master had been out in the garden, and out of curiosity, or for some other reason, he called over to Iron Ass. After no more than a few minutes, the master recognized the state of Iron Ass's mind. "You are passing through zero point," the master said, "It is from this chaos that the true voice can be heard. From this state, the truth can emerge. Sit back and observe yourself. Stop partaking in the mind's debate and think with your heart."

The master took him into the temple where he met twelve monks who had lived for years with the master. There was quite a bit of laughter in the temple, and Iron Ass recalls nothing anyone said made sense. In one case a student asked the master a question and the master slapped him. Another student gave the same question and got a hug. His mind couldn't make sense of the insanity, so he stopped trying.

The master pulled Iron Ass aside and told him his teachings break down the ego and cause the mind to collapse in a sudden explosion, which, in the right instant, will bring enlightenment. His teachings were gradual and by applying paradoxes and riddles to the unsolvable, he would safely ferry his students across the river of zero point.

"A person sits on the shore of a great river and wishes to get to the other side. The thing is, he does not know there is another side, as he cannot see it, for it is too far away. The student has hope the other side exists and he vows to cross the river. Doing so, he steps onto the ferry, and the journey begins. At first he is very attached to the side of the river he has left and wishes greatly to return. As the student grows and he moves farther and farther, the shoreline begins to fade.

"Soon, he can no longer see whom he used to be, as the shoreline has vanished and only the river remains. At the same time, the other side of the river still cannot be seen, and for this reason, the student becomes scared he is perishing. He does not know or remember who he was, or who he will be. He only is. This is the state of your mind. You have led yourself alone to the middle of the great river.

"As the ferry moves still closer to the other side, land can be seen if one is able to focus deeply. Once land has been spotted and the ferry moves in its direction, the mind will have moved through the nothingness. Once the ferry arrives upon the other side, a new mind will have emerged, a new world will follow. The old shoreline can no longer be seen, and it fades into the past. Here, the ferry is no longer needed and it too is left behind.

"This is the journey you have sparked within your mind. I too have made this journey and since I have been to the other side, I can guide you to safety. Once at the other side, you will make a great decision. You can either move onward into the new lands, or you may remain and guide those who struggle on the ferry and on the other side."

Iron Ass said he wasn't capable of responding coherently, yet he understood the master's words. The master was able to clearly comprehend and assess the state of Iron Ass's mind. He was led to a huge meditation hall where other monks were sitting on the stone floor meditating in the lotus position. Iron Ass was directed into the posture and told to close his eyes and focus on one thing. "Look for the shoreline".

In his meditation, Iron Ass said, his mind was filled with nothing but pain and confusion. He sat in the lotus position for three days without moving. The other monks would bring him food and water once a day and they would remain and meditate for three hours with him. They seemed to know exactly what was to be expected of Iron Ass; they had watched many other students make the crossing. Apparently, Iron Ass was taking much, much longer to find the other side. By the second day, the monks began laughing and joking, calling him the man with an ass of iron. They had never seen anyone sit for as long as Iron Ass. By the third day he was simply called Iron Ass.

Toward the end of the third day, he began to see a faint light and he moved effortlessly towards it. As he moved closer, he was filled with joy and happiness. He was still not at land's edge and his state of mind was a delirious joy. Slowly, his mind began to function more clearly until he could hear only one voice speaking to him. The voice spoke crisply, and strongly, and from that day on he has followed the voice faithfully. It has never led him where he didn't belong and he says it is the voice of the Universe.

So that's how Iron Ass got his name. He added the Lone One part because he sees himself as a bit of a rogue. He does things his way. The only thing I didn't get out of the story was what Iron Ass's decision was? I know he decided to help others cross the river; that's why he's appeared to me. But for some reason I feel he never really returned to the other side where he came from. The way he talks, I get the feeling he just hangs out in the middle of the river, looking for lost souls who might need his help?

Nine

DIVINE COURTSHIP

I don't know how I remembered Iron Ass's words so perfectly. Yesterday, when I was writing in this journal, I seemed to hear his words ringing in my ears like some cosmic tape recorder had turned back time, and I was sitting on the sand listening to him again. I left a lot of stuff out of the journal but I got about as close as I can.

It still makes me laugh when I picture that guy, yapping away with his sly smirk on his face, cackling away like a crazed banshee! It seemed he could barely contain himself within his skin. He's plugged into so much electricity I think it started to make me a bit loopy too. Seriously, for a while, I was getting really silly and punch drunk.

The old bag definitely cheered me up with his antics. Just about the whole time, from when he walked up and said hello, until I left, I forgot my problems. It was like going to the comedy club for a night and letting some laughter reach deep inside and rip out what hurts. He completely had my attention. Add to that, at least for a while, the mess of my life looked pretty ridiculous! I must have absorbed some of that from Iron Ass. The guy absolutely glows with that attitude. I'll bet for him, life is one big circus filled with mad clowns and not a care in the world. Only problem with that, I think he's got to be insane, at least on some level. Insanity seems like kind of a high price to pay to be able to howl at the moon and see life as a hilarious divine comedy.

Anyway, I soaked up enough of his energy to last more than a few hours. I actually felt pretty normal for a while there. In fact, most of the day wasn't too bad. I'm fascinated with the old man. All throughout the rest of the day, I found myself suddenly shaking my head and laughing at something he said or something I thought he'd say to me if he'd been spending the day with me.

It wasn't until this morning that I felt horrible again. Waking up was a brutal experience. I felt even if I summoned all my energy and determination, there'd be no way to make it up, let alone face another day of existence.

Long before my wits came to me, I was wishing for night and time for bed. It's those first twenty minutes that are the worst, like waking into a nightmare. I probably didn't move for the first hour. I just lay there with my eyes closed and tried with all my might to escape back into the oblivion of sleep.

Eventually I realized, after twelve hours of sleep, not including a two-hour nap the previous afternoon, lulling my body to sleep was just about impossible. That's when I opened my eyes and tried to imagine something interesting and uplifting to do during the day.

I wonder what Iron Ass does all day? He must have a degree in laziness. In that subject, he's nothing less than a master. I don't care though. Personally, I like him. He makes me laugh, and at the same time, he did say some interesting things.

My problem is I'm starting to feel the same empty loneliness I felt when I first came down to the beach. I dread having to deal with the day. There's nothing to look forward to. There's nothing to hope for.

Once I got up it wasn't so bad. I took a walk along the

shore. I spent a few hours wandering around, quietly watching everyone else, or just lying down resting. I kind of moved from one part of the beach to the next, sitting to rest for a while in each section. There was no purpose or conscious effort to go anywhere. I simply walked and let my feet move me in whatever direction they pleased.

Just when things get their darkest and lowest and I'm about to give up, there is a flash of lightning that lights up the night just long enough for me to start believing that good things are still possible in my life. Like when I watch the sunset. That's the most powerful, but I get these small flashes of light from all kinds of little things.

The nicest thing happened to lift my spirits. A kind lady came by and brought me some food. She asked me how I was doing today and even asked if there was anything she might be able to do for me. Something as simple as a friendly face passing by and saying hello was so uplifting. Compliments and kind words are like rainbows of hope that create sparks within. I don't understand why I'm so sensitive right now. Even the simplest interaction with people lifts my spirits. I think it's this inner loneliness that's creating all the darkness and gloom. In the dark, I can't feel a sense of connection. Maybe I'm isolating myself?

What's breaking me down, over and over, is this slow death I keep reliving and repeating with my moods. They are like the changing of the tides and I'm losing all the trust I have in myself. In the morning I want to put a bullet in my head and after spending an hour with the sunset I feel I'm flying in the clouds! At one moment it's not mentally possible for me to comprehend how life could be anything but a lifelong sentence to suffering and misery. My thoughts are fixated on all the murder, rape, torture, starving children, and just about every injustice that man is capable of. How can I ever find my paradise with all this hell around me?

With all my blessings I probably could live in my own little bubble of safety and happiness as long as nothing bad touches anything too close to me. But even then, my heaven is imperfect. It's tainted by the hurt and suffering of others. Darkness that is very real. I think we've come up with so many ways to justify and explain suffering so we can ultimately feel safe in our own skin without having to really deeply feel and understand what a fragile and sometimes painful experience life can be.

In my sorrows I'm swimming in a giant pool containing all the negative, dark forces that are part of the world. I'm diving deep into the black liquid muck, and I'm realizing the suffering and pain that human beings must endure on this giant mud ball are very, very real. How can I ever escape this fact? Then my life force is gone, hope leaves, and I come as close to death as I would dare.

Within the very same day, I'll be on the beach at Ollie's Peak waiting for the sun's love to shine down upon the water and wake the dead.

"Arise my child! Take up your pallet and walk."

And then I'll feel a warm spark at the base of my spine and within my solar plexus at the same time. My lungs will start to soak in the crisp ocean air, and each breath will feel as if I'm drinking the nectar of the Gods. First the ache in my heart will ease up a bit. I'll actually feel the muscle relax from the contraction I've come to know as *the death grip*. It feels as though my heart has clamped down and is squeezing so tightly that no blood or oxygen can enter and bring fresh life.

The golden light rays on the water and the ocean breeze enter my heart directly like an injection of muscle relaxant. The grip loosens, and once again I can breathe. Long before the sunset begins I'll already have said my thanks and gratitude for the blessing.

The spark within will grow and a toasty feeling will emanate from me. A faint smile will probably appear on my face and expand until I have a pleasant aura around me. The sensation reaches out, spreading, until it's become a loving peace, and then, like traveling from night into the day, my thoughts will shift to the daylight. Like tiny creatures who've been hiding in the woods, the blessings in the world will start to pass through my mind. I'll think of so many wonderful things human beings do for each other. I'll see the love we have for one another. I'll see families having picnics by the lake or couples all dressed in white and celebrating their union. I'll see eagles soaring through the skies and children running and playing in the park. I'll start to feel a pulsating bubble of joy forming in my stomach and I'll feel it float up through my body, up the back of my neck, and it'll burst within my mind, producing little needles of bliss and joy. I'll start imagining what a joyous and wonderful experience life can be. I'll start hoping for the joys and dreams of my childhood to manifest. Not only that, I'll believe my most heartfelt desires are all possible to achieve. I'll even start believing in words like *destiny* and *perfect love*.

After being barraged and flooded long enough with this pure nectar of positive energy and thoughts, I'll let go and easily lift off from the ground and start floating upward. As I rise higher and higher and begin to see the curve of the earth's surface, I'll ask myself about all those horrible and dark thoughts that had just been in my head. How can I feel bliss with all the darkness? I'll be thinking about that, and just when I'm high enough to see the earth as a massive blue and white ball, I'll realize my perception has made the darkness a hundred fold more black and ugly. I'll feel light bursting out of me, flowing into the world, and I'll realize our light within has the power to illuminate so much of the darkness. I'll effortlessly feel life is the greatest of gifts in which we can all live as lights to the world. Extinguishing our own light only acknowledges the darkness.

I'll float even higher, and I'll feel as though I can remain in perfect peace and harmony in any circumstance, in any situation, and in the presence of any darkness. My fear will leave me and I'll realize I can remain in that bubble and still be one with all. My love and happiness become a gift to the world.

I'll float still higher, and at these heights the darkness actually starts to break down as an illusion. I'm not sure if this is a trick of the mind or not, but I'll realize, on the soul level, we are all safe and divinely protected. I'll realize everyone has his path and we can take refuge in that everyone will one day receive many blessings. And then, I'll catch a glimpse of the ending. Memories and emotions will turn into living treasures, and I'll think all is divinely and gloriously perfect.

I'll finally surrender the last sands of hurt I'd been holding between my hands. As the last speck of dust falls back downward towards the earth, I'll reach such a height I can actually hear the songs of angels. I'll see beauty all around me as the most amazing diversity of light-being creatures dance and sing their songs. I'll float just a bit higher and brush the side of perfection, and in those moments, I'll totally lose myself to her divine love.

When my sight and senses return, I'll be sitting right here at Ollie's Peak, staring out into a dark night, trying to catch a glimpse of some light catching a wave as it breaks on the shoreline. I'll be feeling radiant, and tranquility will be flowing from every pore. Maybe I'll sit for a while and try to embrace my feelings in an effort to somehow hold on and never let the feeling leave me. Why do I keep forgetting the love that is all around me? Tomorrow I'll wake, and it will be gone.

Ten

DOCTOR AMBIKA

A doctor of some sort visited me today. At least that's what he told me. I'm more than a bit suspicious. He seemed more like a drug pusher or pharmaceutical salesman. The last thing I need to be doing right now is taking drugs. My balance is fragile enough as it is.

"I've been trying to talk to you for a while now."

"And who are you?" I asked.

"I'm Doctor Ambika."

"I've never seen you before." I told him.

"Oliver, I've been coming by every day since you've been here. You were in pretty bad shape when we first met, but you are getting better. Hopefully the medication is working."

Right away, he started with the medication. Not to mention he's a liar. I've never seen him before, and I haven't taken any drugs, or medication, or whatever he calls it. Still, I played it cool. I had to find out this guy's angle, who he really was, and his purpose. Definitely another piece of the puzzle.

"I'm not sure what you're talking about, Doc," I said, "Do you make it a habit of wandering around here trying to 'fix' people who don't need your help?" At best, I thought maybe he goes around trying to help the homeless.

"Do you know where you are, Oliver?"

"I'm sitting on the beach at Del Mar, where I always used to come when I was young. I've been here a while, mostly at Ollie's Peak, and I'm telling you I haven't seen you once, and I certainly didn't take any drugs from you!"

With those words, a quick surge of panic came over me. Was this man some kind of drug dealer? Even worse, maybe he's a sick lunatic who somehow slipped me some drugs like acid or something. That would explain every single bit, every crumb to the madness.

"Have you been slipping me some drugs every day!" I was pretty scared.

"Oliver, listen to me, please. I'm going to help you focus a bit. I'm Doctor Ambika, you've had a mental breakdown and I'm trying to help you. You're going to have to trust me. I need your help so I can help you."

"I didn't have a breakdown," I assured, "This is so much more. I promise you, I'm having some kind of spiritual awakening, and I don't want you or your drugs messing it up for me. What I need to do is solve this mystical puzzle!"

"Maybe we can help each other solve the puzzle. Maybe I can help you solve the puzzle." he said," Don't you feel cut off somehow? Can't you tell something isn't quite right? Oliver, I've dedicated my life to helping people like you 'solve the puzzle' and live as healthy a life as possible. If there's a chance I can help you, isn't it worth it?"

The doctor made a good point. I'm sure I don't have to figure this thing out by myself. In fact, I'm sure God has many people working for him. Look at Iron Ass. It seems he was put here just for me. That couldn't have been a coincidence? The only problem is, for every person who's here to help me, there's probably a counterforce that is working to confuse me and make sure I don't solve the riddle.

"Oliver, lets walk back along the time line a bit. Relax and let's go back to January 24st. Can you remember that night?"

"Yeah," I said, "that's the night of *the dream.*"

"How were you feeling that day? Were you tired or filled with a lot of energy? Do you remember any troubling thoughts or feelings of special-ness?"

"I can barely remember that long ago, Doc," I said, "I don't think I felt much different than I had since the ritual."

"Oh, a ritual? What was that about?"

"Just my fraternity's initiation," I told him.

"Had you been feeling different in any way before this initiation?"

"Well," I said, "the semester before was pretty stressful, but I felt ok for most of it."

"But you did feel different after the ritual? How did you feel?"

"Sometimes I felt light and airy, and other times I felt a bit down," I said, "It's hard to describe. My mind seemed to drift around a lot, and sometimes it was hard to focus. Do you think the ritual was some kind of magic? Or do you think that maybe it opened a mystical door to other worlds!"

"Tell me about this ritual Oliver."

"I can't," I said, "I've been sworn to secrecy."

"Were you allowed to sleep? How much food were you given? How long was the ritual? Did you have to do lots of physical exercise? Were you kept alone? "

The doctor started pinning me down with one question after another. He was writing little notes as I answered the questions.

"It was about a week long, not the ritual though. We barely slept, didn't get much food, and we kept busy the whole time."

"And what about the ritual," he said, "What went on there? This is very important, Oliver. I have to tell you this could be the trigger. In fact, I need to know what went on at that ritual. Did they deprive you of your senses for any period of time?"

"You'll have to use your imagination, Doctor."

"What about the ritual? What did they say and do?" he asked again.

"I told you. I can't tell you. Not any of it."

"Oliver, do you realize your sanity might depend on this? You went into this ritual with a latent mental illness that somehow was triggered."

The conversation wore on me. Maybe this doctor really was trying to help, but he kept badgering with one question after another. It started to get more than a bit confusing. I told him I was getting tired, but on and on he went. Maybe he's the one doing the hypnotizing? Who knows what I told him?

He had me so tired, I was drifting in and out of awareness until finally, he let up with the questions. That's when he started pushing the drugs. He hated it when I called them drugs.

"They're medication, Oliver. They are the sole reason you're getting better. You've got to give me some time to figure out what works for you and what doesn't. This is no easy thing to figure out, what you'll respond to. It's serious business."

"But I'm not taking any drugs!" I yelled," They change the way you think, the way you feel, and the way you act! How do I know you're not the counterforce, trying to keep me stuck in this dream? I'm escaping right now, and maybe you're worried about that, and these medications are just the thing to keep me here. You're acting like all that's happened is a terrible thing!"

"It's an illness, Oliver."

"How do you know?" I said," Maybe it's a blessing? The sunset speaks to me! I feel the love-bliss of God! Poems come to my lips from an inner well without effort! Sometimes I want to fly to the heavens in praise of such beauty! Why would you want to take that away from me?"

"Because it's not real. You are suffering, and you don't even realize it. I'm not your enemy, Oliver; medication isn't your enemy. Your enemy is delusion. You already forget about the terror you've been through. Do you remember the first night we met? You were so scared and miserable you were ready to kill yourself. Right now, you need medication to help you see reality as it is. Do you want to be here forever?"

How can this guy be expected to understand the graces of God I've experienced? Why would I expect him to think any differently? To him, the possibility that something spiritual is taking place is not an option. Without that possibility, he has to find a solution outside of that realm. This alone prevents him from solving the puzzle.

"Doctor," I said, "Please try to understand. How can you expect me to see reality clearly when you want to put me on drugs, or medication, or whatever it should be called? Why do we have to discard the possibility that I can figure this out without medicine?"

"Because the longer you stay in this state, the worse it is for you. It's like you've moved into an enchanted castle. Right now, the castle has you under its spell and you don't realize it. The longer you live in the castle, the harder it is to come out, and the easier it will be for you to slip back into the castle."

"Well, maybe I want to live in the castle," I said.

"Do you really want to live alone, inside yourself, with nothing but hallucinations and voices to keep you comfort? Believe me, Oliver, if you could wake up to the truth, you'd never want to come back here. In fact, I'll bet for the rest of your life, you'll do everything in your power to stay as far away from the castle as you can."

"I doubt that very much," I said, "Obviously, you've never heard the sunset. You've never heard the voice of the siren. If you did, you'd know she's irresistible, and when she calls a soul to her castle, to her castle you go."

"That's just the kind of talk that worries me, Oliver. It reflects how far you've gone into delusion. In a way, you're right.

Each time you visit the castle, it becomes a little easier to return. Right now, you've traveled on a dirt path. If you keep it up, one day you'll have paved a super highway, and whenever the wind blows, you'll find yourself locked up in the castle."

"So now you're telling me I should fight against the beauty? Your counsel is to turn my back on the gift given me?"

"Oliver, when you get better, you'll know I've told you the truth. You think you're swimming up but you're really going deeper into the waters. You're too deep to see clearly, and at this point, medication is what you need to stabilize."

Those last few sentences struck a chord. *"Deeper into the waters"*. The words echoed in my head. Am I going deeper? Do I need to go deeper? Is the doctor right or is he against me?

"I've got to tell you, Oliver, right now I'm not sure what has happened. It could be a psychotic break, but time is against you. If you can't get out of the castle within a few months, this might look more like schizophrenia. It's already moving in that direction. At the same time, you've got quite a few signs of mania. You've been writing like a madman in that journal of yours since day one, and from what I've heard today, it very easily could be bipolar illness *. Even then, the quicker you get well, the better."

"How long would I need to take the medication?" I said.

"It's too early to tell, Oliver. Maybe for life."

For life. I pretended to finally agree with him. He would have argued with me all day and never left until I agreed anyway. I stopped fighting. I stopped talking about the sunset. I stopped trying to explain the spiritual wisdoms that were being revealed to me. This made the good doctor happy, and he gave me a cocktail of at least four or five pills. Of course, there's no way I'm taking them. I'll never put that crap into my

---

* In brief, Bi Polar illness is considered a mood disorder in which a person may swing from depression to elation.

body. Once I do, the whole thing is out of my hands as I see it. Right now, at least I'm the one in control, not some drug. I'll pretend to take the pills and see what kind of information I can get from the doctor. He's got half the puzzle anyway. I'll learn what he's got and figure out the other half for myself.

Eleven

THE WAY TO LIGHT BY FOCUSING ON LIGHT

I really like talking with Iron Ass. He lifts my spirits and helps me forget the seriousness of my troubles. We talked for a while today. He was laughing and ranting and raving as usual, but also he came across as a pretty genuinely nice guy. He's obviously a product of the sixties and all the hippy stuff must have stuck with him. He simply has a good time.

Probably most people don't take him too seriously. The hat alone would make most think he's nuts, and maybe he is, but at the same time, he's got some interesting things to say. I guess he's kind of a rebel maybe. He makes fun of all the things most people take seriously. In fact, just about everything is a bit of a joke to him. Sometimes he makes sense, and other times he doesn't, and even though I think he knows when no one can follow him, he keeps right on going, laughing and talking. It's like he's got a million inside jokes with himself or somebody. Every time he makes one of those jokes I feel like some part of me should be laughing too but it usually goes right over my head.

I told him about meeting the doctor. I thought Iron Ass would have steered me away from modern medicine. He surprised me there. He seems rather indifferent.

"Hell, do what you've got to do! That's all I'm saying. Maybe the Doc can help ya, and maybe he can't. Get it! Ha! Don't ya see Oliver, you're allowed to use all the tools that are available to ya. That's the exercise. That's the ritual!"

"You mean I'm allowed to use whatever I need to solve the puzzle?" I asked.

"Well, what if you don't have whatever you need? Ha! What you can do then is use what's available to ya!"

"Iron Ass, the doctor wants me to take medication," I told him.

"Hell, in the stone ages they had to rub sticks together to get fire! Tools, Oliver! Tools! One day those doctors will understand there's more to it than what they can stick their microscope in. Yeah! Those old buzzards are only doing what they know. Get it? They're offering the best they got. That's why I always counsel to see the *divine physician* who can heal all things."

"So are you saying I should take the medication?" I asked.

"I'm saying what I'm saying, whatever that is! That's for sure. Look, you're one whose feet seem to lift off the ground. Your heart longs for the heavens! That's a great thing! Your task is to stay grounded through the whole experience. Get it?

"Maybe you are one of those who can find balance by applying the natural laws under strict discipline? Maybe the extra ballast of spiritual truth will be enough to right the sails! On the other hand, maybe you'll need to use all the tools laid before you? That's the task before you then, isn't it! Yes sir! You've stepped into the enlightenment chamber and all you have to do is maintain balance while life comes at you. That's the middle way baby!"

"What the heck is the enlightenment chamber, Iron Ass?"

"It's the ritual of life, Oliver. It's the riddle you've got to solve somewhere along the way! You get it then? That's what this is all about. The goal is the ultimate, and the path has been blazed. But we can't touch the goal, can we? We can find it, and live it, and be it, but touching it is a tough one.

"The paths are blazed by the great masters who have paved the way to the gates, and in their love, they return like a candle and light the way through darkness. We follow the ideals in our heart and they lead us along the path, sometimes brushing the edges and other times losing sight of the path. Each person's path is his own, and none are the same yet we may follow the same light. Yeah! It's as simple as that! We're all on a path whether we just go in circles or not.

"What you're looking for, then, is the infinite. This is moksha and its meaning is liberation. Liberation from anything which distances us from infinite awareness, infinite bliss, infinite being. Oliver, it's God you're after, the ultimate prize for the truth seeker."

I have to say, energy was rising up as Iron Ass was talking. The sheer excitement of hearing I really am on a divine, spiritual quest, was enough to start me dancing and singing! "So it's true then? I am on a vision quest?" I asked.

"Oliver, in the name of love, many have discovered this secret buried deep within. They found it under layers and layers of rust and dirt where no one could see it. They found it was like the moon on a cloudy night. It was always there, pure and glowing, yet the clouds had hidden its secret. Finding the key is simply a matter of removing the rust and blowing away the clouds. Then the rays of light will shine constantly!"

"This is incredible!" I yelped, "It's like everything I've ever hoped for actually might exist! How do I unveil the secret?"

"Every day, I want you to practice the art of silent communion. Yes sir! It's within the silence that your mind will grow still, and in that quiet, a deeper voice may be heard. As it is now, a great storm is sweeping across the surface of your mind, and in the noise and confusion, you're cut off from the deeper self. The idea, then, is to transcend the surface and sink into the depths where the waters lie still. That's where serenity lives and a greater power sleeps. It contains the energy that heals body and mind."

"But Iron Ass," I said, "I've got to live in this dream. The answer can't be simply to escape life itself? Can it?"

His answer was more of a sugar-induced sermon.

"Hell no! Hell, hell no! What you've got to do is use the inner voice to transform the dream. So here we are, and here's my point. Fix those filters on love and enlightenment! Yah, that's it! Exactly! Ha! You do that, and then you take it to its extreme, and you can take any experience and fill it with joy.

"What it is then is the way to the light by focusing on light. It is the road to the heart by focusing on the heart. It is the path to heaven by focusing on heaven. The meditation is simple and straight forward. Wear glasses that filter the experience of life through a sieve of love. Love can be found anywhere and in all things God created. It's your task to unmask the beauty held within all there is.

"Ultimately, life becomes what it is meant to be, a meditation on love. From start to finish and cradle to grave, life itself is a meditation within a dream. I'm telling you, Oliver, you do this, and you'll see your life change! You'll be like the shape shifter, like the shaman, changing the nature of reality through your perception. The power is in your hands. The choice is yours. Hopefully, you won't choose to become crap-like. Hopefully you'll choose to become God-like."

That's it for me, that's all I needed to hear. I'm sold. My desire to conquer and understand life is raging. What are we doing here? What's the purpose? I can't seem to grasp the answer, but the wheels are spinning with a fury. I *can't* wait until the end to find out, I have to know now. It's all I care about. Every night at the sunset I'll say a prayer for someone to watch over me and show me what I'm looking for.

Twelve

THE PERFECT PATH

I can't believe it's only been a couple of weeks or so since the dream. I guess that's a while but things were so hazy back then, the memory has aged almost to where I don't re- member. It's like I passed through an illusion and I've emerged from its veil with most of the experience erased.

Looking back towards that night, it appears as only a flicker in the distance, creating the effect these past days have taken eons of time. I sometimes catch myself looking for the spring bloom even though we're still in the middle of winter. The weather is nice though. The skies are sunny and clear almost all day long. It makes for perfect days at the beach, feeling the warm sun on my skin and waiting for the sunset. For the rest of my life I'll go down and watch the sun sink into the ocean in all its glory and colors.

I've been practicing the meditation Iron Ass was talking about. Right after I take my walk down along the shore, I sit in the sand and picture a white rose. He's right; my mind goes all over the place, almost to the point where I can't sit still. I just relax and try to maintain a gentle focus for about twenty minutes or so, and then I'll open my eyes and I'll think about the things Iron Ass has been telling me.

It really is funny how all I seem to want to do is solve this mystery? I used to think about things like grades, money, fancy cars, and big houses. I worried about what kind of job I'd get down the road, how I looked, and what people thought of me. I wanted to do something important, to be a respected person, to accomplish things that impressed people.

Now I couldn't care less! Nothing matters until I tap into this secret Iron Ass talks about. Every cell in my being is on fire, ignited by this burning desire to comprehend the mystical realm.

In two weeks my entire world has been turned completely on its head. I wanted big parties on my private yacht! Just goes to show how truly long each click of time has been! Everything has changed. I can almost understand and relate to the way Iron Ass must feel. Never in my wildest dreams would I have thought that might happen. To the rest of the world he looks like an unmotivated, lazy old dropout.

Right now I can almost understand why he wears that sly smile on his face when he's talking. I can see it in the gleam in his eyes. He realizes what people think of him and that little smile is because he's got the key to a golden door within. He really does share an inside joke. The joke is on all the outsiders who look down at him feeling superior with all their outward accomplishments and trophies. I'd be laughing too!

To me, right now, there's only one thing that matters and that's cultivating this inner kingdom of love, devotion, and service that few have discovered. What an elusive path!, sometimes appearing and then fading right before the eyes. It winds through our lives connected by a magical fiber tying all our experiences, thoughts, and feelings together in the perfect mix, creating the world that unfolds before us.

The more I think of it, the more I'm convinced Iron Ass is laughing at all who are blind to the truth about life. Really, everything else is just a sham we get caught up in one-way or another. Power and ego are roadblocks or diversions that keep us from discovering all the little secrets just waiting to reach out and call our name.

When I look back, I can see a silver fiber interconnected through all my life's experiences. It's amazing! I can't believe I've never noticed before. There are so many coincidences and chance encounters that didn't seem to have any meaning. Everywhere I look I can see road signs helping to point me in the right direction as well as countless diversions that kept me traveling in circles over and over until finally, I caught on, learned what I had to, and moved forward. People like Iron Ass don't just accidentally come into our lives; they are universally brought there! If that isn't the exact opposite of everything we are ever taught! That's what's so amazing and incredible about the truth. That's what makes it so funny! Most people are really wandering around in their own delusions.

I think I've finally awakened to the first degree of *the secret*. We are all on a spiritual and magical journey that leads through countless kingdoms and experiences! If we trust and open our eyes to this truth, the first veil splits and each day we can wake with the sun and treat it as an adventure into higher and higher lessons of love. Look around at every moment. Pick it up and hold it close. Examine it. Everything is unfolding according to where we are and what we are seeking. People who cross our path are all there for a purpose, whether they are a close friend or a momentary acquaintance.

Sometimes the person passing by on the street with one kind word is the bearer of a very important message. We need to be looking and listening closely for the wisdom and magic that life will bring to us. How does that saying go? Have an open heart and open mind and you just might learn something.

I'll admit, the veil is very tough to unmask, but really, it doesn't have to be. What I'm saying is we don't have to pull it apart to see through the experience. Let it wear its mask. Do

we have to see through the dream to know we are dreaming?
Why not enjoy the dream, accept it, and learn from it? Rising
above the illusion and looking down upon it and seeing the
millions of silver chords that have been woven together to
form reality is an incredible experience, but what I'm saying is,
it's much easier to flow with the dream and simply be aware
while we live it. There really is a divine creativity weaving a
web around us. Like uncountable numbers of atoms all ar-
ranged in a structured agreement, our life's experience is part
of a larger intelligence. We are experiencing our own world in
a dreamlike bubble.

Is my dream the only real one? Is everyone I come into
contact with just characters in my dream? Are they all in my
world as actors playing their part to teach me something or
lead me one way or another? Am I the only real character or
are all the characters a part of me? What about the birds and
the trees or even the ocean or the desert? Are they all part of
my dream?

I think the only answer dabbles in genius. Yes, they are all
actors in my dream, but I am also an actor in their dreams.
Yes, the ocean and desert are part of my dream, but they are
also part of everyone's dreams. The birds are not only mine,
they are everyone's. I am real, and everyone is real, but we are
all so magically mixed with larger and larger bubbles of dream
that ultimately we are all the dream itself. The magic and most
incredible display of creativity is the force that synchronizes
each and every individual life with all the others. From my
best friend all the way down to the person standing in front of
me in line at the grocery store, all are the result of a synchro-
nicity which is everywhere at all times. When my world reflects the world of another, we are very close. I may turn the
corner, and there they are. If my world is so different from
another, we may never meet. If we do, however, it will be no
accident, and our experience will be interwoven with divine

creativity.

I think the creativity linking all, that is everywhere, in all things and all experiences, is God, Spirit. If we realize this and trust, the dream doesn't have to break down for us to take advantage of the magic. We don't have to be some mystical seer or prophet to benefit from the cosmic milestones and signs given to us each day of our lives. We simply need faith and a good heart.

Funny, it's just coming to me now. Maybe Iron Ass is smiling because people treat him like an eccentric nut because he doesn't care about the distractions and absurdities of life. To those who build their lives on those things, he'd have to be a nut. It's the only way to justify their world without dealing with their own illusions. It's the opposite that's really true. Just because most of the world is caught up in mass hypnosis doesn't make it the truth. No wonder so many things look funny from Iron Ass's side of the fence. People are staring at him through the notches in the fence, laughing like he's some trained monkey, and he's looking back with his sly smile and seeing that they are laughing at him within a cage.

I do understand Iron Ass's smile. It's not a smile of superiority or judgment. It's more like "I know something you don't know". Or maybe at its most extreme, people will be laughing at him with delight and he'll reply with the smirk he wears with such childlike abandon. Those times it'll be saying, "The joke's on you, fellas".

I feel like the dolphins that swim along the shore and play in the waves. They're so pure and free and filled with a serene inner smile. For them it's their natural instinct and place on the earth. They flow with life, the waves, and the tides. Their lives are simple and uncomplicated by meaningless diversions that most people assign high levels of importance. Their whole existence seems to be a lesson in shining a light of joy and tranquility to a world that has forgotten. Whenever they swim by and play in the waves it stirs a content in my belly that sloshes around like I've just finished a good-sized mug of ale. With their liquor in my system so many worries and concerns of life shrink, and many disappear completely. The small things don't seem like that big of a deal anymore. They become what they are, just tiny frustrations that really have no business taking up my time, concern, and peace.

My choice is to swim with the dolphins and even one day I aspire to fly with the eagles. I can clearly see the golden path before me. Iron Ass has helped me realize this path has always been there. He has helped me accept the path is real, which is like opening the greatest of gifts. I feel an enchanting journey calling. I plan to answer that call. I think one day everyone will hear the call. I hope they'll answer it. If they do, it'll be interesting to know that one day, I stood in the same spot and heard the same call. I hope they'll find me high on the mountain where the trail has become covered with white snow.

Thirteen

THE PICK-AXE OF DOUBT

"Who is this Iron Ass?"

The question startled me but I knew the voice. I looked up and sure enough, there was Doctor Ambika, talking as if we were in mid conversation.

"Iron Ass?" I said, "How do you know about Iron Ass?"

"Well, for the last forty five minutes you've mentioned his name at least four or five times."

The doctor can be hard to follow. Sometimes he comes through vaguely clear and other times his words seem to echo from a distance. Once in a while, it's almost like he's not really there, or maybe in another instant, he'll suddenly be speaking to me. This was one of those times. He knew about Iron Ass so he must have been right, possibly we had been talking for a while already.

"I'm not too sure who Iron Ass is," I said, "I think he must be some type of guide sent here to help me."

"I was hoping I wouldn't get that type of answer, Oliver. To be honest, this magical thinking is at the heart of the problem. Your imagination has taken over in place of rational judgment. These thoughts of special-ness are part of the illness." Doctor Ambika informed me.

He went on. "The sunset, the mystery, and even this Iron Ass are all products of delusion. Your mind has you trapped in a hypnotic grip.

"It is very common for people in this state to think they are in touch with some special truth, secret knowledge, or realization of divinity. You think you have uncovered a veil that held you prisoner in a false reality which others see as real."

The doctor knows some things which I'm not sure how he can know. "How do you know so much about the way I feel?" I asked.

"I've been working in this field for many years, Oliver. We've found that people in your condition often tell a very similar story. We've mapped out some of the common characteristics and they help us to diagnose or identify what may be going on in a person's mind."

"But I know whatever is happening to me is a spiritual event, " I said, "I can't describe the feelings and energies that come over me. There really is a secret hidden beneath a veil, and right now, I can feel it."

"These thoughts and feelings of special-ness are a chemical mixture in your brain," said Doctor Ambika, "They are delusions of grandeur. The mind is out of balance. It's almost like it has created its own high."

"Yet all the spiritual teachings I've studied apply perfectly to the situation I'm in, " I responded, "Every piece of scripture is written in the same light that I'm in. They all make perfect sense! How do you explain that?"

"Loose-association, Oliver. It's also very likely many of the scriptures were written by people in a state of chemical imbalance. Right now, you are able to take any piece of information and bend it and twist it until it reveals something magical. The ordinary suddenly hides the fantastic. This discovery creates elation and more neurotransmitters fire away.

"Oliver, I have to stress this as deeply as possible, and this may be hard for you to understand. Stay away from the spiritual quest. Stay away from Iron Ass as well. All this type of thinking is like throwing gas on a fire. You are in the fight of your life."

"Doctor," I said, "It's my belief in God that is getting me through this. You're trying to take away everything I believe in!"

"Belief in a God is a wonderful thing, Oliver. What I'm saying is that now is not the time to be studying religion. Do you know one way we can tell if someone is improving or slipping backward? By the amount of time he spends talking about his divine revelations or spiritual secrets, and by how emphatic and animated he is about them.

"All I seem to do with you is listen to stories about a mystical journey and special knowledge being given to you. For someone in your state, these are only signs of delusion. Right now, the religion you have studied has become real. There is a danger in that, Oliver, which you don't see.

"An illness becomes a temptation by the devil. Hallucinations take the form of angels and demons. Every word you've read in your bible becomes energized and takes life. That's the reason you believe this breakdown has to do with God. Your mind is out of control, and because of this, you are experiencing extraordinary things. It's only natural for the mind to try to rationalize and explain what it perceives and why. For people who have studied religion, it's predictable their experience takes on that structure as an explanation."

The doctor was on a roll, and making some points too.

"If you put yourself in the midst of the bible or whatever else you have read, you're going to spin your wheels over and over while the true cause is simply chemical.

"Don't you see Oliver, the spiritual quest is merely the 'spin' you are framing your breakdown within. For someone who is

110

unable to tell fact from fiction, you are setting yourself up for a battle with a fictitious entity brought to life by delusions of grandeur, and then you're trying to battle that phantom and all the personal meaning it holds for you. Religion for someone in psychosis is a gamble, one that might send you straight to your own personal hell.

"How does that sound, Oliver? A bit scary, isn't it? Maybe you're sitting here torturing yourself in your zeal when the truth is you have a mental illness?"

I have to admit doubt had been creeping slowly in my direction. It brought tiny daggers of fear as well. Maybe I was crazy? What if God wasn't watching over me? What if things weren't destined to work out? What if there wasn't a God? Then I'd really be scared. What if I really, truly, was deluded, and while I thought I'm awakening, in reality, I'm someone, broken, and still in the midst of that breakdown?

The peace and calm that were held together by my non-wavering belief in the ultimate spiritual truth broke down, chipped away by the pick-axe of doubt. How horrible would a fall from such a height be? In one instant, to think you stand at the very door of heaven, in the next only to slam into the rocks and caverns in the lowest crevices of the earth.

On went the doctor, "Oliver, when you've regained your senses, these thoughts and feelings will be gone. You won't be able to imagine or comprehend how they could have seemed so real."

"How do you know that?" I asked.

"Because that's how it is for everyone. At least the ones who make it back."

"Maybe," I said, "the ones that come back found the truth, only they couldn't handle it, so they had to forget. Maybe the others don't come back because they escaped."

"Whatever the case, Oliver, we still don't know which group you fall into. If you don't let go of these delusive, religious, thoughts of special-ness, maybe I won't be able to help you. Maybe you won't be among those that make it back. And yes, maybe forgetting is the only way to heal from something so intense.

"Remember what I said, Oliver; you are at a crucial time. What has it been? Weeks now. The longer you're in the castle, the harder it is to get out."

Then he looked at me in a strange way. "Don't read from that little book under your bed!" That really struck me. In fact, I've thought a lot about it. Maybe he knew I would? After all his talk about staying away from spiritualism and religion, why would he say something like that, in a mysterious way? How does he know I always keep my bible under my bed? How could he know that?

Maybe he knows this is a spiritual quest. If it is, then he's leading me astray. Of course, he could have said those things, worded them in a mysterious way, because he knew he'd be speaking on my level, that way they would have some bite.

What if this is a dream, like Iron Ass says? Whom do I trust? I have to admit, Iron Ass could be crazy. If he is, maybe it's just like the doctor says, some people crack up and never make it back.

I'm afraid the quest has been taken from me. My thoughts tell me I've hinged my hopes to an illusion and followed the guidance of a man whose heart broke too deeply, leaving him to wander the beaches in a fairytale where the pains of reality are forever banned from existence.

Fourteen

THE ROBBER FEAR

*I*ron Ass is one strange bird. I stayed up all night thinking about him and what the doctor said. Just when I think he's a very wise and intelligent but eccentric man, the whole thing has to fall apart. I've lost most of my faith in him. How could I have bought into all that "dream" talk? He really had me in the middle of his own ball of delusions. If we want to, I think we can convince ourselves to believe in just about anything. It's easier than it seems really. It's like a form of self-hypnosis we reinforce over and over until it becomes our reality. That's the deepest brainwashing, the kind where we use our own mind as the guinea pig. It just goes to show how incredibly dumb people are capable of being. Look at me. I've been down at the beach for a while now, and I'd gotten to a point where my imagination was so powerful I actually believed the sunset was speaking to me! Not only that, I've been wandering around trying my hardest to feel love and bliss emanating from plants and trees.

I really thought the ocean was sharing some kind of healing love with me! Now that I'm snapping out it, it's more than a little scary to me. I've already been wandering around talking to the birds and trees and pretty little flowers! What's the next level in the insanity?

I have this joke I've been thinking about. It's this little inside joke I had, and in way, I shared it with Iron Ass. I kept imagining everyone else was crazy. I thought they just didn't get what life is really about. I thought the sunset speaking to me and the ocean's healing love were the true reality. I figure that's what Iron Ass was trying to tell me. What it really is has to be the ultimate delusion. How could I have let that guy lead me away from sanity so easily? I think it's because he did it so gently and slowly. He planted his little ideas and gave me all these little exercises and then he sat back and let me do this to myself. He's the one that's crazy! He wants to suck me into his world and convince me everyone else is insane. That's the real reason he's got a sly smile on his face! That's what his joke is really about!

The doctor's words keep repeating over and over in my mind like a broken record. The more I think about it, the more I can't believe what an ass I've been. At the pace I was going it wouldn't have been long before I reached level two and started holding conversations with the rocks and nature spirits who like to play around the beach. Jesus! I think I just about completely lost my foothold in reality! It's like I was walking right over the edge of a cliff and into the abyss. It really, really scares me. I've got to stop listening to all the voices in my head and pay attention. One or two more steps and I'd be living in Neverland!

Maybe that's what it's all about; the imagination rises up and soon enough all the poems and fairytales you've ever read suddenly become real. That must be level three or something but I think I was closer than I want to know! Once you reach that deep in the jungle, the trip back has got to be some form of hellish torture. Imagine that; the creative faculty of the mind grows so strong that it takes precedent to logic and rational thought. Every possible thing you might be capable of imagining has at least a breath of life within the bubble of delusion. And that bubble is pretty much infinite because there are no limits to the imagination! Anything can exist in that state.

From day one, Iron Ass has been trying to take me by the hand and lead me out of the world where normal people live and into his kingdom of insanity where imagination alone creates the illusion. He's just lucky his mind is full of all that "feel the love" and "flower power" type of thinking. Take another person and lead him into that kingdom and he just might find himself scared half to death! I know I am.

He must be an intelligent man, but I can't imagine he doesn't have any less than a screw or two loose. He definitely is smart though. I can see exactly what he's been doing. It's like he takes my mind to the gym three times a week and he's focused in on some very specific muscles. He works the mind over and over with the same thoughts and ideas and each time I go to see him again, those muscles are just a tad bigger. Once he's stretched the imagination far enough, even his babble seems to make sense. That's when the feet start to leave the ground and imagination starts to weave its web. The mind is so damn powerful! It scares me. I mean I was out there talking to the sunset! Not just talking to it, I believed with all my heart and soul the ocean heard me and understood what I was saying!

Believe me, once you realize how insane your thoughts are, it's not a pleasant feeling. I was actually trying to imagine that some great master could actually levitate above the ground! That's how bad the insanity was getting! Iron Ass had me contemplating the idea that somewhere out there, there might be a spiritual genius who could defy the laws of physics! The scary thing is I thought it might be possible! I thought a completely enlightened and ascended master probably could walk on water. I didn't care about a damn thing anymore. I convinced myself I'd be happy living under some bridge as long as I had food and water to nourish my body. If that isn't self-deception then I don't know what it could be? We can convince ourselves of anything.

Iron Ass thinks he's found the answer but really he's living in the self-created illusion of heaven, that's all. He's convinced himself he's happy all the time. He's convinced himself of just about everything he believes in. His entire world has been created from all the things he's ever hoped for and everything he's ever wished for. He might think he's happy, but where the hell is the reality in it all! That's what I'm saying.

Yes, he did make some observations I've never thought of, but really, when it comes down to it, they're all coming from his world of delusion. He's always preaching. I feel like this guy wants to suck me into his world of "the dream" and all the other illusions he keeps saying are all around. He says the mind creates an illusion around everyone within "the dream" but really, he's the only one in the dream! The rest of us are all living outside in reality where things make some sense.

Most likely, he's a man who slowly lost touch with reality and he's hanging on by just enough rope to make him appear as if he's sane. Isn't that weird, how someone can have just the right mixture of intelligence and insanity to sound as if he has a wisdom beyond our comprehension?

That's what scares me. After everything that's happened, I'm still not sure about Iron Ass. I still have this little voice inside that says he might be right. That thought alone scares me too. To me, the fact that I still entertain the idea sounds too much like believing I'm talking to the trees. It's a very unsettling place to be. I think he's stretched my mind far enough to the point where it will never go all the way back. That's what scares me. It's like he pried a door open and no matter how hard I try I'll never be able to completely shut it.

Honestly, I do wonder that maybe someone has been able

to walk on water. I do wonder about those nature spirits and the tree's love and the bird's song. The sunset's music seems too real for me to fully accept it as only my mind's imagination flexing its muscles. I don't know whom to believe. Who can I trust? I feel I can't even trust myself. After all, only yesterday I was talking to a beautiful wildflower I passed on the cliffs. What I've got to do is hang out with people I trust, with my friends whom I've known since I was a little kid. At least I know who they are; they've got nothing left to hide from me. These other people I just don't know about. And Iron Ass, I can't understand him. He's spinning me around in circles trying to confuse me. He doesn't ever just come out and say what he means. He plays a game with my mind, and I'm too confused to understand the game. He's playing a chess match with my head, and he seems to always be one step ahead. If he wants me to go left, he might steer me to the right and I'll go left thinking I've got him beat only to learn that he wanted me to go left from the beginning. Where's the trust? These are people to stay away from. I'm done with Iron Ass. Right now, the thought of letting him program more of his teaching into me makes me nervous. It scares me.

What sucks is I know something has me hooked. The desire burning in me won't let me stay away. I'll just have to be careful and figure things out for myself. Just because he says something doesn't mean it's not coming from his own crap. That's the truth. Maybe he did say something smart when he told me to stop listening to other people's garbage and listen for my own inner voice. Of course, I doubt he thought I'd apply the scales to *his* teachings. The bottom line is this: (in fact, I think Iron Ass said it himself) either he's found enlightenment within the coke bottle or he's just about the craziest son of a bitch I'll ever meet.

I do know this: I'm taking the medication the doctor brings me. This illusion, this Maya, or whatever it is, is too difficult to see through. Maybe it will help. I took the first dose last night. I couldn't take the debating in my head anymore. Maybe I'm thinking more clearly already. Maybe that's why I'm not so caught up in "the dream", Iron Ass, or even the mystical puzzle. Maybe it is delusion?

Fifteen

SURRENDER?

This has been the absolute worst week of my life. At least it's almost over. Last week was like a slow death march that sucked the life from me in a rhythmic and methodical way. It beat on me one blow at a time. What a cruel torment. Why not show mercy and deliver the deathblow? Instead my love is squeezed from me in tiny droplets of tears, one by one until all that remains is this lifeless shell I live in. Even now I can feel the constrictor tightening its grip around my chest while allowing just enough air to keep me from slipping away forever. Today is the first day I feel alert enough to write since taking the medication.

It's not enough to take my life, the real goal is to break my will and shoot it's dagger into my heart. It seeks to enslave my spirit in its miserable world of darkness. It's so cold in this place. I can't take it much longer. This slow death is agony and it's been so carefully and painstakingly planned, almost to perfection. I've been brought to the very edge of the abyss, and with all strength bled from my being, I'm given just enough nourishment to escape death. When all seems lost, I'm thrown a crumb. When there is no hope, I see a faint light in the distance. When I cannot bear one more instant of pain, the death grip loosens just long enough for a breath of fresh air to fill my lungs.

I don't know how I got to this point. My hopes and dreams have disappeared so quickly. I wish I could go back to being like everyone else. There doesn't seem to be any way out of this thick muck of despair, no way to turn around.

I hoped the medication would help me to finally escape all the B.S. and crap I've been battling. For a while, I really thought it would work. I miss the sunset. I even miss Iron Ass a bit. Maybe he's not so dumb? Whatever connection there was with Mother Nature and God is gone. It's been a week since I started taking the medication; they're a whole rainbow of pills. I'm lubed up on every drug imaginable. Whatever the dosage is, it's as much as any mortal man can take! At least my problems used to be only mental. Now, my body feels miserable. I'm tired, I can barely look into the day-light, I feel weak, agitated, and my muscles feel as if they aren't a part of me. Add to that, my brain seems to be crawling at the pace of a turtle.

I'm worried I made the wrong decision. Maybe I fell right into the trap? Maybe the doctor doesn't know as much as he thinks he does? Whatever momentary happiness I had, it's been removed. I feel like my better half has been taken away. At least I had the sunset and the ocean's bliss to comfort me. Now they're all gone. The sun is silent and the ocean has lost its glimmer. They're not even as real as they used to be. Wonderful sparks of joy used to bubble up at times, and they're gone too.

If it's impossible to be in hell when God is with you, I am now in hell. The God with me in this nightmare has been drugged. There is no God here, only insanity. I can see I'm crazy, I realize that. The joy of my search for truth, my vision quest, is nothing but the wish of a heart that wanted to believe so badly. My belief in a love watching over me, sculpting this dream to perfection, could have withstood any hurt, any tragedy, and endured to the end. I took the medication and hoped so much it would fix all my sorrows. The doctor made it sound like magic dust. Whatever it did, I feel I'm worse off than ever.

I haven't talked with Iron Ass since I took the pills. Maybe I'll go back and say hello. There's not too much I'm sure of. I miss the songs and the sweet stories I used to hear. Maybe that's a good thing? Maybe not? For all I know the voice of the sunset might have been my saving grace. Maybe I heard the song because I was very close to the answer? Now I've moved so far in the other direction, the distance has become too great. Then again, maybe I was on the brink of insanity with Iron Ass in the distance screaming for me to take the plunge. Maybe reality is taking hold and starting to solidify?

Sixteen

SOMETHING TO BELIEVE IN

Doctor Ambika spends a lot more time with me now. He keeps telling me I'm getting better every day. It's become a mantra and I'm a bit sick of hearing it. I doubt very much I'm getting better. I think I may never get better.

Every time we talk now, he runs down a standard list of questions. "Any thoughts of special-ness? Any racing thoughts? On a scale of 1 to 10, with ten being normal, how is your mood?"

"My mood is horrible. You've eliminated the highs and left me with only lows," I said.

"Well, it takes some time to figure out what medications work and their proper dosages. Maybe we can add a mood stabilizer to the mix."

"Please no," I said, "I've already got too much of this poison in my body as it is. This agony is twice as bad as what I was going through. Now I can't tell if I'm feeling bad because something is wrong with me or if it's because of the medication I'm taking."

"Some of the side effects will go away over time. If others are a major problem we can find something to counteract that. What's important is that you are finally showing some improvement. You're getting better every day now."

"How do I know if I'm getting better?" I said, "If you're sitting in my skin, you'd be praying for things to go back to the way they were."

"Oliver, I told you coming back wouldn't be a piece of cake. Right now, the dosages are high because we need to put out the fire as quickly as possible and prevent any flair ups. We can try to make it as comfortable as possible and later we'll reduce the dosage when you've been stable for a while."

"I don't think I can take it much longer."

"In a month you'll be feeling better and in a few years, maybe this won't matter anymore."

"Doctor, what happens to my mind if I take this stuff for years? Maybe this is brain related, but maybe that's the part of my brain where spirituality lives? Maybe the neurons or whatever have gone a little haywire, but maybe I'll be severing my link with the divine if I keep taking these pills."

"You'll still have plenty of creativity left if that's what you mean."

"What I mean," I said, "is that maybe a portion of my mind has been activated which sleeps in most people. Maybe I simply have to learn to control it? I'm worried I'll be silencing a gift."

"There is a price to pay for a healthy mind," ended the doctor.

I wonder what my heart thinks I should be doing. Have I been given a gift? Is the price I have to pay periods of sadness and uncertainty? The choice is mine, and I feel I want to choose whatever God's will may be.

I think of Iron Ass talking about the divine physician. God can heal anything. In truth, I don't think this medication is working. I think it is making me less of a person, someone numbed up so he won't feel anything too deeply.

I think I'll take an honest look at what I believe in. I have to decide whom I'm going to trust. I have to choose because I realize I can't make it on my own. I need help from someone who can see clearly. The only one I've ever completely trusted is God, and that's really what Iron Ass says to do. I'll just have to trust that God is really watching over me, whether this is a dream, a nightmare or reality, he's with me and he'll bring the right people to help.

I feel so much better with that tiny bit of faith restored. I don't know how to endure without the love of God. I hope the spark of faith will never blow out again. It seems like it's being tested over and over. Maybe when I've passed all the tests it will always blaze inside me.

I know one thing: it was a mistake to remove God from the picture. I crumbled so easily. To let go of the very thing carrying me, the strength that kept me afloat, or at least fighting, was the biggest mistake I've made so far. I know God was with me in the good times and the bad times. He was there through all the joys and the sadness, all the right turns and even when I'd turn from him. To erase him from the picture ruins the whole painting.

The way I see it, I've got two forces pulling me in different directions. For whatever the reason, both have a tremendous amount of power over me. Call them insanity and reality, light and darkness, good or evil, or whatever, I've got to make a choice. Which voice am I going to follow? I can't go on moving in both directions.

Seventeen

TRUST IN THE RIVER

I snuck up to Iron Ass as quietly as possible. All I could think was I'd somehow let him down or betrayed him by staying away the last week. I showed up early and sat down hoping Iron Ass wouldn't ridicule me for being a walkout, I know how sharp he can be. I felt he'd see right through into the dark depression I'd slipped into. One quick glance would tell the whole story. I had no idea what kind of reaction he'd have or what he'd do or say. The whole thing had me feeling real nervous and unsure of myself. I felt like a little kid who'd just been caught with his hand in the cookie jar.

As it turned out, all the worry was for nothing. In fact, I'm really glad I said hello today. It's like I chose to show up on the perfect day. He was yapping away almost before my butt hit the sand.

"Hey Oliver, where the hell've you been? Can't say we haven't missed ya, but I'm sure glad you're back here with the rest of us monkeys! That's all that matters anyhow, right now. Forget the past, and while you're at it stop worrying about the future so damn much. All that stuff will take care of itself. All that matters is the present moment and how you think and act in that moment. Got it? Ya!"

"Nice to see you too, Iron Ass," I said, "Sorry I haven't been around for a while. I've been having a hard time figuring out whom to trust."

"Listen carefully, and trust in this," he said, "Right now, in this instant and whatever instant may come, your feet are walking upon just the kind of ground they are meant to be on. Whether it's shit or shiny you've got to realize and trust that creation has placed you just where you need to be. Get it then? If you're not here, then you're there, and if there is where you are then that's just the damn place you need to be! So don't second-guess why you're there or why you're here or what the hell you're doing there in the first place! Who the hell knows all the answers anyway? Just be glad you made it here. That's the true accomplishment and if you figure out that here is always somewhere, then why would you have anything to worry about?"

"Iron Ass," I said, "It seems like I've got more than a lot to worry about. Whether I like it or not, I'm caught in some sort of battle and I'm afraid if I make one wrong move, one step in the wrong direction, I'm going to lose the fight."

The old buzzard was in fine form. His answer was flying out of his mouth with lighting speed. "Why fight the battle when it's not really real. That's what I'm saying. Surrender! Surrender! Not only that, there's nothing to surrender to anyway! The real lesson here is *trust*. You've got to start trusting because you're sure as hell going to learn the lesson. That's for sure. And let me tell you one thing: you sure as hell don't want to be taught that lesson. Just claim it now in this instant, and live it. That's the best way anyway. The other way is the rocky road and it's a real ugly sucker. That's paranoia! Hold on to that long enough and sooner or later it'll break you into submission."

"But whom do I trust?" I asked, "That's the problem. If I trust the wrong thing, it might be the end of me."

"Trust in what you believe in," he said, "Look at it this way: there's a crystal clear river flowing through our lives. We can go wherever we want and do whatever we want on this river. Wherever we go and whatever we do is just fine, because it's all the same river and it always ends up in the same place. Some people like to swim upstream against the current and others like to shoot the rapids. Me, I like to float on the surface, relax, and surrender to the current. That's a hell of a place to be. The river takes me here and there and wherever it takes me and in whatever moment it may have taken me there, as far as I'm concerned, divine timing has worked its magic, bringing me to the perfect place in the perfect instant."

"You make it sound so easy.\," I said, "but what happens when things go wrong?"

"Hell, Oliver! There's been more than a few times I've spilled over the edge of a hundred foot waterfall and just before I crash back into that river and all the rocks below I'm sure as hell cursing the damn thing! Now when I hear water pounding down in front of me, I'm swimming upstream like a lost tuna!

"What I'm saying is this; trust in the universe doesn't mean you're gonna wake up each day in some lush garden of peace and happiness. Some days are gonna be like waking up drunk and in the trash dumpster outside your condo! Trusting doesn't even mean that anything's gonna change!"

Sometimes his logic baffles me, especially when it's dispensed in the midst of his cackling and yipping and yelling. "If nothing changes, then what's the point?" I asked.

"Well, of course it changes, it changes everything, but really the rest is the same. What I'm saying is that whether you trust or not, the day is going to be the same. It's in the perception of trust that you can surrender and accept what the day brings. If you can truly trust that the spirit of God is watching over you and helping to create each day in your life, then how the hell could anything be wrong?"

Sometimes I think Iron Ass refuses to see the truth. "How can anything be wrong? Are you kidding?" I said, "How about living homeless at the beach, half crazed, and feeling like death?"

"That's because you're not trusting, trusting everything is being taken care of just the way it's supposed to be. It makes things so much simpler and easier than having to second-guess every thought or idea that passed through our little minds!"

He said the last part with a twinkle in his eyes. "Maybe things aren't what they seem? Why not wake up each morning with the perception that all life asks is that you live the day as fully and wisely as possible. I'm telling you to treat each day as if it's a gift from the Gods! Each day is like a newborn baby born in complete purity and freedom. Might take ya a while to get there but I wake up each morning and watch the sun rise up over the mountains in the east, and for me yesterday doesn't even exist anymore. All that's real is the day ahead of me, and if it turns out things don't go my way, no big deal. I try my best, and I'm true to myself and if I can stay in that place all day long, I'm satisfied with whatever the hell might happen. I wake up real early the next day and wait for the sun-rise to bring me a whole new life! How incredible is that!"

"Iron Ass, those things work just fine for you because you really don't give a damn. You can wake up each day and be happy with what it brings because you don't want anything! The rest of us have things we want and hopes and dreams and all kinds of stuff that takes some serious thought and work to get."

"That's just great as far as I'm concerned!" he yelped, "If you want something, then go out there and get it! I don't care. I'm sure not stopping ya. While you're out their 'getting' all that stuff, you can still trust you're exactly where you're sup-posed to be and doin' exactly what you're supposed to be doin'. That's all I'm saying. Problem is, most of you guys get caught up and lost in all that "stuff" and before you know it you're in over your head - not to mention most of the stuff you're after is a bunch of rubbish anyway, but who am I to tell ya what you want. Only you know, but it seems like you haven't even figured that one out yet either!"

"So what's your secret then, Iron Ass?"

"What I want just happens to be the same thing the river wants me to have!" he revealed, "That's the trick, and it sure as hell isn't an easy one to learn. Surrender and trust is what it's all about. The less you fight the more peace you find."

"But what if the river seems to bring nothing but misery?" I asked.

"What I'm sayin' is, I can trust that the river has brought me the right things. I'm not happy when I find a snake at my front door, but I believe and accept it's there for a reason. There's a reason for most everything, and there's a cause for every effect. If that's the case, and I believe that spirit is creating the river, that spirit is the river, then anything can be turned around and made into a positive experience. Doesn't mean you're better or worse than before: it only means that something can be learned from anything. Don't be confused by that one. Too many monkeys are just happy when the sun shines and withdraw into mourning and isolation when it rains. That's one hell of a ride to step onto!

"Ha! Laugh now, but that's the ride you've been on! Things go your way and you're happy, and when things fall apart, you're sad. What a crap house that is!"

"I sure would like to get off that ride," I said.

"If you're sick of the ride, then my advice is to get the hell off it! You do that by surrendering and letting creation play its part in your life. For a crazy old bat like me, my job is to just live the dream. I accept what the river brings me. I do swim around a bit now and then, but that's just me doing my part.

Hell, for all I know, whenever I'm huffing and puffing swimming up the stream, that's just what I'm supposed to be doin'. Never try to out reason or out think the Divine! That's for sure. Yeah! I'm always one step behind reaching for the carrot."

"The shaman is a wounded healer, Oliver. And that's ok, just fine and dandy! It's his wound that gives him his power. That's a tough one to get but when you do, you'll see what you have is a gift."

Eighteen

RISING OF THE TIDES

I've been thinking about yin and yang. For a while there, I had this sensation of a force growing within but it seemed to come and go before I could act on it. A rising tide within grew until I felt totally uplifted and motivated to go out and kick some ass in life. The tide came in at least once or twice a day and took me to a nice place. It's almost like two different people living inside me. The one riding in with the tide is just about the most joyful, carefree little guy I've ever met. He's all smiles and so full of optimism and raw energy. Whenever he decides to come in, it's like all the good things in the world creep out from under whatever rock they've been hiding and do a little mambo. Worries fade, mountains turn into piles of sand, and even the air seems laced with humor. The dumbest little jokes or comments are just about the funniest things I've ever heard. The energy and excitement would have me feeling real social. I'd think about calling old friends and pretty much just getting out there and being with people. Words effortlessly came to my lips and I felt so comfortable in my skin, a bit like stepping into a mild alcoholic buzz. My mind felt greased and lubed while the world was firing on all cylinders.

The feeling is already starting to return. The energies are waxing and waning, so to speak. The air has a hint of intrigue. The magic of life is emerging. I was a fool to throw this away hoping for a quick fix from pills. After my talk with Iron Ass, that was the end of medication. I'm trusting what I believe in. Of course I'm not letting the good doctor in on it. The last thing I need is to hear another voice pulling me wherever it wills. I'm too easily influenced in this state anyway.

At least my mind has sped up again. Now I can think. I've got a flood of possible solutions moving through me. Maybe the yin energy is rising up and trying to spill over into the yang? I almost have no choice about that either. When the tide comes in, there's no way I can sit around lounging, or sleeping the afternoon away. The waters contain too much bubbling, bursting energy to sit still and do nothing. I end up going out and I do all the things I've been wanting to do. Maybe I take a jog or stop and talk to people for a while. The more I think of it, it really is like another person sliding into my body and taking it out for a spin.

The problem with the tide is it hits a low a couple of times each day also. I've gotten so used to the daily waxing and waning of forces, I've forgotten about the struggle, even though I've been living it. The free spirit riding in on the waves leaves just as smoothly as he arrives. What happens then is all the nature spirits and happy thoughts that were dancing and singing disappear into some hidden magical forest, and I'm left alone in a totally different world.

The difference in my mood isn't that the tides of love and mercy have somehow changed and become sad and lonely: it's that the ocean is no longer there. That's a profound difference and that's why it feels like a totally different person. I think differently. I'm more adventurous, and I have a genuine love for life when the tide is in. When it's out, it's like the bridegroom has left the building and a lonely and quiet chill is the only tone remaining.

I think this waxing and waning of the tides is somehow tied to the yin and yang energies. The rising tide I feel is the water growing in force and trying to spill out over the dam and into the next world. As far as I see it, I've got to learn to consciously direct that stream of conception and birth. Those waters are meant to flow like a river but I've been keeping them trapped in the valleys behind self-created dams in an effort to feel safe and protected from drought.

What's happening now is the dams can no longer hold the waters, and as they rise with the moon and other forces, they are spilling out in bursts of energy, followed by a depression as the flow of water becomes blocked once again. I've got to figure out how to ease the pressure and find the perfect balance and flow for the energies of the river.

I tried to explain about the yin and yang to Doctor Ambika today. He was kind enough to listen, and for a while, I really thought he was understanding. Here I was, revealing a deep secret about something he considers to be a mental illness, and the truth is, it went in one ear and out the other without a single cell processing the insights. I wanted him to realize the fundamental cause of my imbalance was due to the presence of certain energies. Since he's a doctor, I felt my insight could help many people who are in the same condition as I. If only he would have listened. What seemed so ridiculously obvious to me meant nothing to him.

As our talk wore on, I started picking up on Doctor Ambika's demeanor. My sensitivity was in a pretty heightened state and I could tell from his eye movements alone he had no intention of hearing my message. What he was doing had nothing to do with my words. He was analyzing me. I can still see his eyebrow arching with suspicion as I let the words flow. *Never cast pearls before unbelievers*, I thought. The doctor was sizing me up. I could feel an alarm going off somewhere within him.

This time I wasn't going to let him wipe out my spirituality. I'm a bit wiser now to the whole game. As soon as I realized what was going on, I shut my mouth. No more insights for the doctor. He doesn't want to hear them anyway. He did his best to get me talking again though. He baited me with questions of a spiritual nature and tried every trick he's learned over the years. A few times he managed to get me pretty excited because he seemed so genuinely interested in the yin and yang energies. Still, I held my ground and did my best to keep my mouth shut and pretend I didn't have access to any extraordinary information and I assured him I wasn't having any "thoughts of special-ness". I downplayed the yin and yang as a passing idea.

I know Doctor Ambika left with concerns, but I think I gave a pretty good performance. I know the ritual by now so I told him exactly what he wanted to hear. Another slip, and he'd probably have doubled my medication. Guess that doesn't matter since I'm tossing that crap down the old toilet. I know I can beat this thing. I didn't know what was happening to me before, but now I've got a boatload of experience. I've got enough ballast to make it through whatever storm is out there. I just have to believe in myself.

Nineteen

RETURN OF THE SUNSET

The sunset tonight was the best yet. Not just because it was so beautiful, but more so because she is speaking to me again. It's unbelievable!

Today is heaven! I woke in the morning with the sun, ocean waves crashing in front of me. There's something about living on the beach. I'm starting to jog along the beach every day now.

Everything seems to be clicking all at once. I've got so much energy it's hard to sit still. I want to get out and live. It's like every beat of my heart squeezes some kind of drug through my system. All of a sudden life has potential.

I wonder what sparked the change? All I know is my depression was like a fog around my head. Now it's gone and I'm so much lighter. Iron Ass is right, it's all mental! Before, all my thoughts were negative and gloomy and now I'm letting go of that misery. I'm thinking about the good in life, the beautiful things. I was too caught in the darkness, convinced any good this world had to offer was nothing more than simple distractions providing momentary sanctuary, helping us forget. Now I know negativity is the illusion. The world is either as dark or as light as we make it. I saw the world through eyes tinted with sorrow, so everything looked empty and meaningless. Now the tint is gone, and I see there's plenty of wonder to live for!

I'm living in a beautiful place on the beach. I can swim every day. There's so much to look forward to! I want to be with people. I want to share the joy of life, especially with those who are passing through the same waters that were killing me. I wish I could feel like this all the time.

Now I know why Iron Ass said the quickest way to change the world is to change your mind. Just put on a different pair of glasses and everything looks different. Now his crazy talk makes more sense too. "The world has changed but it's still the same." It's my perception that has changed. We see the world through our own filter. Sometimes the filter gets a bit dirty, and it distorts things.

I'm still not quite sure what made the change? I've definitely been filling my mind with knowledge and positive ideas but I thought these changes are gradual. Maybe it's the meditation I've been doing.

"If the brain chemistry is balanced, then peace and energy will fill your mind"

Right now I feel perfectly balanced. Maybe that's it. Through my wandering I've found myself right in the middle, right on the line between left and right brain. Moses parted the seas of left and right brain where his enemies couldn't follow. That's where I must be.

"The pendulum is swinging. It swings back and forth until it finally comes to rest in balance. The poles shift back and forth until they find even ground. The poles are shifting."

Maybe the pendulum is moving from darkness to light. Now I've found the optimum amount of light for my being. I have plenty of energy. I feel wonderful. I want to be with people. I want to be part of life again! I feel more and more alive.

"*Balance is the key*"

I wonder how much light I can take? How close to the sun can I get? I think I once heard that in the Bardos, worlds between worlds, if a person gets too close to the sun he becomes a crazed God. I think maybe that's the same light I brushed the night of *the dream.*

"*The light of love heals all wounds.*"

The pieces all seem to be coming together now. It all makes sense. Some people have the capacity to endure so much light, they can actually merge with the sun. They completely lose themselves in the loving energy, and then they return. These are the enlightened ones. My problem was I hadn't prepared body and mind. We have to train in order to receive the highest blessing. Most of us are at different levels of light. We expand and contract and expand, always trying to move closer to more and more light. Everyone has his own balance.

If you fill a container with water, eventually it will overflow. The secret is the container must expand as the waters grow. The enlightened ones must have understood and mastered this process. A container cannot be suddenly twisted and pulled into a larger container. It will break and the water will spill. The container must slowly expand. Our capacity for love must grow. The gift of life is a process allowing our capacity for love to expand, if we choose.

Only love can be present for the final ascent. The great ones increase their capacity for love by practicing the art of love, love for everything - love for the flowers, the trees, and animals, for all people. At the same time, they purified their minds. They filled themselves with only loving thoughts.

Why couldn't I see these things before? They seem so utterly obvious now. Whatever veil hides these secrets from us is dissolving before my eyes, leaving a glimmering world of unmasked mysteries! Perhaps I'm about to make the final ascent. The time I've been here has been a kind of preparation or training to enable my soul to manifest and blaze unchallenged within this body temple. That makes perfect sense. Of course my mind would have to undergo some form of restructuring. That's probably what the doctor is talking about. New pathways had to be blazed within my mind. For whatever reason, instead of being gradual, the whole thing exploded all at once and blew my mind. Now I'm getting used to the changes. It's taken a while to acclimate, so to speak. The way I think, act, and feel have all been changed, almost like a different entity is stepping in, and we're blending together to form a new and more harmonious pattern. Whatever is happening is clearly a process guided by an intelligence inherent within the fabric of life itself!

Twenty

ONENESS

"Oliver, your mind is sowing the web of a false reality. These insights, perceptions, and sense of clarity are purely delusional. Loose association, combined with the imagination, is presenting explanations in your mind's effort to rationalize what is happening to you. These secrets seem real purely by the power delusion has over you."

Doctor Ambika hasn't come by for a few days now. As far as I see it, that makes things all the easier. It's hard to hold on to faith when someone constantly chips it away. If it can't be captured in a test tube, then how can it exist?

Even still there's a voice questioning my every thought and action. I must have imagined the doctor's words today? It's like a few seeds of his doubt took hold and sprouted in the fertile soil of my freshly cultivated mind.

Oh well, the past is behind and I'm moving forward so rapidly I never intend to look back! The days seem to be going by faster and faster now. I can hardly sit still and write for too long. I'm not buying into the B.S. anymore and I'm feeling better and better all the time! Momentum really seems to be building. Every minute now I'm feeling more and more energy, more alive and filled with life. If this is what Iron Ass has been selling, I'm so glad I finally bought it.

Life is more and more enlightening every day now. I'm understanding just about anything I put my mind on, which is a miracle in itself. Even Iron Ass's speech seems to have slowed. It's like I'm right there with him, waiting for the next word to come off his lips. I'm getting sharper and sharper. Maybe it's because all the cobwebs are finally clearing out of my mind. Who knows and who cares! I'm just having a good time each and every moment! The little things don't matter anymore, and add to that, I don't have any big things to worry about either.

People have become so friendly and outwardly nice, I've made a ton of friends. I feel I've opened the door on a hidden paradise, and all my hard work is finally paying off. I'm hearing the sunset louder than ever. Whatever it is, it's soothing and warm. Its voice reminds me of an irresistible siren calling out from the oceans.

The sunset's music makes me wonder about sensitivity. As the sun sinks into the deep blue ocean, I become sensitive enough to hear and feel the beauty in all things. There seem to be degrees of sensitivity and connection. When we meet people and find they have common interests and similarities, we feel a connection to them. When we hear a song or poem that strikes a similar note in our heart, we feel a relationship, a connection to that song or poem. The connection is there because we can see a part of us in that poem. Likewise, we can see a part of ourselves reflected in other people. Whether we choose to or not, we feel that connection to certain degrees. The connection reminds us that we are not alone.

On another level, what if we were able to see the beauty in all things? Seeing this beauty reflects back our own inner beauty and a connection can be made with the flowers, the trees, and forests. If one is sensitive enough, it is possible to feel the beauty of colors and experience that connection.

Feeling the beauty of a flower is very subtle, much like reading a poem that strikes your heart. The connection is the same though, one of reflection. If only we could learn to open ourselves to the beauty and love which is all around us. I can feel the sunset again because I've fine-tuned my sensitivity. I've opened my ears to the divine melody playing throughout the universe. In a state of heightened sensitivity, I can say without doubt that our own love is being reflected back to us in every given moment. There is not one thing of beauty in this world that doesn't contain a part of us. We need to learn how to open up, to hear and feel the music once again. I wish I could tell everyone what I'm feeling right now. What a wonderful gift that would be! The truth is all around us. It can't be a lie or an illusion, because I feel it too strongly.

Twenty - One

THE SECRET SOCIETY OF LIGHT

There are enlightened ones that walk among us, people who carry the light of the sun within, and they are considered sacred and holy by all in the spirit realms. They live their lives and endure the same hardships and joys as the rest of us, but deep inside they have the purpose of bringing light to the world. As more and more children of light come to this world, the darkness will be replaced by light. With every person who expands his capacity for light, dawn moves one step closer. With every person whose love dies within, the dawn retreats. The earth is waxing and waning, preparing for her ascent.

The realization hit me like a bolt of lightning. It's like I'd been wandering around in the desert for years, and then one day, someone opened a gate and I stepped into a world filled with inexhaustible treasures. There are many worlds within worlds and there is no question I stumbled upon a new community I never knew existed.

I wonder just how many people out there are carrying this secret with them? I discovered a community who dream of the same things I dream, and in the blink of an eye, I wasn't alone. I was a sheep returning to the flock in a great celebration.

I kind of wonder if that's what the inner circle is like. Magical doors open, and suddenly you're invited into some esoteric labyrinth filled with secrets, magic knowledge, and brotherly love. From that point on you return to the world but you carry a knowledge that bonds you to all those in the inner circle. From time to time you stumble upon others who have also made the journey, and even if you've never seen them before, the connection is there.

That's exactly how I feel. Everyone is so friendly, warm, and funny, plenty of personalities! Man, what a bunch of characters! I've stepped into a heavenly realm. At least that's the way I picture it.

With open arms and smiles on their faces, the souls of beings of light welcomed me to paradise. Honestly, it was one big family, that's how comfortable I felt. I spent the day laughing and talking with each and every person whom creation brought to the beach. I was telling stories, singing songs, and some people had tears in their eyes they were laughing so hard.

Where did all these people come from? Are they just like me when they're back with the rest of the world? I can't figure it out. It's like a masquerade ball when everyone takes off his mask and reveals who he really is. Have these people been walking amongst us in the cities, silent to the light and sacred knowledge within?

I'm seriously wondering if I've been let in on the most guarded secret in the universe? Maybe there is a whole community of people who are awake to the dream of life. They actually know we are children of God, divinely blessed and protected as we walk through life. We are all brothers and sisters, and for some reason, these people live in a state of joy and clarity because they have found the kingdom within.

I don't know if I'm crazy or what, but all day long while I said hello and talked to people, I had to fight the urge to ask them if they "knew". I wanted to say, "Are you Awake?" So many seemed to have a gleam in their eye that said they carried the secret, but I was too worried to ask. They might think I was crazy if I did.

I'm really wondering just who is a part of this club, the inner circle. It seems anyone around us could be carrying the secret. I wonder if the great poets and composers were all a part of the secret society. Maybe people of the circle are in every facet of life, quietly and dutifully performing some sacred task or mission, the mission to teach by example.

I might be crazy, but it feels like the whole day was created for me, like it was the welcoming party that came to greet me as I walked into the circle. Those of the community of light were summoned and came to give blessings and reveal the secret I've discovered. I'm pretty sure Iron Ass must be in on it too. And probably all the people I've met on the beach lately, they must be a part of it. No wonder they were so nice to me; they were watching as I approached the gates! They had the delight of sitting back and watching another move through the same passages that led them to the circle.

I can barely contain myself! All I've dreamed has come true. There really is magic! Life really is magical! We just have to awaken to it! There really is a loving and kind earth that exists! He who seeks shall find! The kingdom exists, and it's like a giant secret only revealed to those who find it for themselves. They'd think I was crazy if I went around telling every person I met.

I'm so high I can't believe it! I have to go and tell everyone what I know, but they'd probably lock me up if I went around talking about a secret society of light bearers who walk the earth awakened to the inner kingdom of heaven.

I see what they're doing. They go about their lives, living with joy in their heart, and exist as an example of living love. They are reflecting the kingdom to a world that has forgotten. You can't just tell a sleeping person to "wake up!!!" I doubt that would go over too well. He wouldn't understand. Instead, those of the circle wait till asked, and only then do they reveal the wisdom they hold within. "Ask and you shall receive", "Seek and you shall find", "Knock and it will be opened"! I finally understand what that means; I've lived it! It's true! It's true!

I wonder how many people are awake and how many are asleep. It's amazing because everywhere I look right now, I see things screaming out the secrets of the kingdom. There are messages all around us, yet we don't see them. The messages must come from those who have found the circle. Fairytales, songs, poems, movies, stories, so many tell the tale of the kingdom, and I guess that's the only way they can be told.

I don't know if I'm crazy or not, but I'm telling you there are children of the inner circle all around us, and they go through life with that secret inside them. To play it safe, I'm going to shut up about the kingdom, but if anyone asks I will tell all I know about the secret community that turns dust into gold.

Twenty-Two

WORLD DESTRUCTION

I haven't slept for three days now. I've got way too much energy moving through my body. What's happening to me? So many ideas are passing through my mind, and life appears faintly dreamlike, softer, less real. I seem to be the center of some huge event. I'm hearing poems and music. They're not just poems either. I've been hearing stories about different worlds and realms of creation where only the spirit can travel. I listen all night, and during the day I'm out jogging or talking to God. It's become a frantic pace. I wonder if people notice what's going on inside me? Am I getting paranoid? What the hell is happening?

I couldn't figure things out so I went to see Iron Ass. I can't understand one thing he spit out.

"Beautiful day today, isn't it?" he said.

I had no time to talk about the day. I needed answers, and so I jumped right in with my questions. "I don't know what's happening. It feels like my whole world is shrinking."

I'm not sure what Iron Ass meant, but I was glad he seemed to understand what I was talking about. "Ah, worlds collapsing upon themselves, going from large to small, many to one."

With so much energy surging through me my voice must have been shaky and unsteady. "Iron Ass, I don't understand what you are saying to me?"

Iron Ass kept right on with his dialogue. "Well, you must be able to. That's how you got here, isn't it - worlds collapsing upon themselves and other worlds springing up. Isn't that how the universe works? It expands and expands at light speed, and then crosses a threshold and collapses into itself. Isn't that what has happened? The mind has collapsed and expanded into a new world, and now it is collapsing again. Your universe is compressing into one cell containing all and then, upon crossing the threshold, it will again expand to infinity. It's how you crossed through the doorway to begin with. If only love remains at the point of death, then the new universe that emerges will contain only love."

"Iron Ass, I can't figure out if you're crazy or enlightened or what!"

I don't think Iron Ass even heard my words; he just kept right on talking. "Your world is becoming more and more condensed, and in that contraction a universe will die and be reborn."

He was right there. I've been having too many crazy ideas. Sometimes I think that everyone around me is an actor, playing some kind of part. The whole show is centered on me, and everything people do and say is somehow designed to help me heal in one way or another. I know they have their own lives but I keep feeling something special is centered around me, like everyone else is in on some kind of process designed specifically for me. I've been fighting the urge to ask people if they were "in on it". I'm so lucky I didn't, I'd have looked like some kind of lunatic!

Maybe all Iran Ass's talk has made me crazy too, all that enlightenment stuff and the weird answers and explanations he has for everything. I finally got my nerve up and asked him what I've wanted to ask for so long.

"Are you enlightened or are you just totally crazy?"

Iron Ass just sat there laughing and laughing and laughing.

"No, seriously, I have to know because I can't keep this up, I think I'm starting to lose my mind."

"I am enlightened to the illusion that is all around you."

"What the hell does that mean?"

"You will find out soon enough my friend. In that time you will realize truly that the world around you was and is a direct reflection of your beliefs and desires. The mind creates your reality. It can create worlds from the ground up in an instant, complete with past, present, and future. What you choose to open yourself to becomes real. Like the Christ you could have said to this mountain 'move' and it would do so. This world is governed solely by the mind and its perceived limitations. All is an illusion."

I was already full of confusion when I went to see Iron Ass and his counsel left me totally lost in the woods. I had to get the hell out of there before I couldn't think at all. "I'll see you later, Iron Ass. Thanks."

"One more thing, Oliver; it's very, very important. Have you heard of the turn-around point? The waters are bottomless, buddy."

Much like the rest of our meeting, I didn't know what the hell Iron Ass was talking about.

"What do you think enlightenment is?"

"I don't know," I said.

"Well it sure as hell doesn't mean going crazy or experiencing some drug-like buzz! That's for sure. Look, let me tell you a story.

"There was a very respected and honored saint. One day a glorious angel appeared and said he'd come to lead the saint up to enlightenment. The angel held out his hand, and as he did so, the saint kneeled down on one knee and searched his heart.

When he looked up he told the angel he was not worthy of such a precious gift. At that moment the angel transformed into the Great Tempter, the source of all delusion and Maya itself.

"Listen to me, Oliver because I speak from the heart. Maya is calling to you. He's holding out his hand to lead you away. Use all the tools you've been given by God to see through the lies. Find God in the ordinary not the extraordinary. Graces may come but magic is not the goal. Stay grounded in reality.

"What if enlightenment is waking up to the realization that much is not as it seems, and God is with us always? Enlightenment is more like taking a deep breath of pure, clean oxygen and feeling so refreshed. By the way, I may not see you again, Oliver. It's all over."

The last crack sent me right over the edge. I thanked Iron Ass for his advice, which was about the most meaningless stuff I've ever been told, and I got the hell out of there. I got to Ollie's Peak as darkness fell and I've been trying to figure out what's happening to me. The energy at the beach is too powerful. I feel like a sponge soaking it up. Thoughts and ideas are coming to me in flurries. Poems are filling my ears, and I can't even write them down because they pass so quickly.

The world is moving too fast now. Sounds and noises are really starting to freak me out. The buses going by sound like ghosts moaning and crying out. I tried to read in this journal but I can't get past the first paragraph. I keep forgetting what I've read. Add to that, it seems to be written in some kind of code too.

I can't believe it, but I don't think the world around me is real. Nothing makes sense, and time isn't the same. I keep having these flashes where I'm in some kind of ward or in my room at school, lying on my bed and staring at the tapestry hanging above my bed. Other times I'm back at my initiation. This world isn't real: I know it. Where the hell am I?

Am I dead? Am I in hell? My mind is moving faster and faster. I can't keep up with my thoughts anymore. I can't figure out where in time I am!

Maybe this whole thing has been a dream? It must be! A guy named Iron Ass and secret societies of light! Why didn't I figure this out a long time ago? I know this isn't real! Let me out! Let me out! Maybe somebody has me hypnotized or something and they're playing with my head? I'm locked in some artificial hypnotic world! Who is the hypnotist? Is it God himself? Let me out! I've figured it out! I've solved the puzzle! Let me out! I solved the puzzle! Let me out! Please God, let me out! I know this isn't real anymore!

Twenty - Three

THE LAST JOURNAL

I am sitting in the innermost room of a majestic palace. Surely this is the home of Divinity, the dwelling of the Lord. On this day, in this moment, my dream has been realized. I cannot describe the stillness of mind nor fathom the unquenchable peace that flows through me even now as I effortlessly write these words, as if they flow from my heart and into ink as a waterfall gently trickling into one world from another. To experience life in this nakedness of mind is bliss. Not a thought, not a doubt, not an iota of a ripple is upon the ocean of my mind. Am I dead? Only the awareness of heart remains.

As I look out, the crystalline palace soaks in light and merges with the light itself, becoming transparent. I find myself gazing out into the heavens, like the Gods on Olympus.

I keep waiting for the experience to break down, for a thought in some form to stir from out of the unborn, undying, fields of azure blue that shimmer, pervading all I experience.

So calm, so peaceful, so effortless is my existence. To think the day would end here in paradise is to imagine oneself waking from a nightmare in which every hope and fantasy had been slaughtered and into a joy revealing the dream an illusion.

I was sitting at Ollie's Peak, caught within the walls of a broken mind, when I heard the melody of a flute. The morning sun touched upon the waters and a shimmering road appeared on the glistening sea. The flute called me to walk upon the waters, a perfect path. Words filled the air in writing of liquid light.

"The dawn has arrived . . . Within yourself, within your mind, its many oceans and cities, there is a door. Behind this door lie the garden and the Lost City of Angels. Once in the garden, you will find three doors. It is behind these doors that you will find what you seek. Countless men and women through the ages have searched the darkest caverns and highest peaks fueled by a burning desire that somehow cannot be quenched. For those who understand, this is the quest for the grail lost so long ago.

"In humble dedication and astute determination those who were scattered and fled from these hillsides search in an effort to find The Door. The mind holds within itself countless doors and passages. Each of these doors will have its day. You see, each door contains self-knowledge that must be reckoned with. Each of these doors has been carefully sculpted and designed by the mind itself, and if you seek to deceive yourself, you will only stumble and fall or be led astray.

"Some doors hold the warm beauty and loves of past experiences. Their energy is warm and soothing. Be forewarned that within the entire realms of the mind, from east to west, from north to south, across the oceans and the skies, there lies only One Door that leads to the Garden. 'Those who find it are few'. "It is the door of love. Know at any time you can call upon your faith and God to be your protector. When faith leaves, hold on to hope, for it is the seed of faith. Be humble and kind, and always carry your love close to your heart. It is your love that has brought you here. Do not fear it.

"Your door lies within and its color is green. All the tools and supplies necessary have been given. Here we think with our heart. There are many paths to this door and many worlds within the garden but through this door everyone must pass. You have all of heaven's blessing and protection. Only love lives within the garden, and only love may pass through the door and into the castle. For this reason, only love can remain."

Time suspended, lost, yet the moment was over too soon. I was filled with such energy and burning desire. It was all I could do to keep sitting instead of running straight onto the ocean's path. Far on the horizon, I could see the silhouette of a giant mountain. I knew my path lay ahead; nothing could hide that from me. The mountain reached to the heavens and clouds thickened around it, but the light of the sun did not dim.

The sun was high in the sky when I began my ascent. Gathering all my faith, I took my first step and found the water supported my weight. Streams of golden light formed a path along the water, streaking in a prism of light.

Several hours later I had climbed to quite a height. The ocean melted into a painting of forests and valleys canvassing miles and miles. The trees lining the valleys and the meadows were a brilliant green. All below blended into a deep green carpet of living landscape. Just ahead, green turned to a shimmering white as mountain snow appeared on cliffs jagged crevices. The mountain climbed still higher where its white peaks disappeared into a fluffy white cloud ceiling. The clouds glowed from the sun above, forming a ring of light.

In time I entered the snow line. Here I sensed a change in the mood of the atmosphere. The feeling and sense of past were an overwhelming burst of nostalgia, almost as if the snow and cold had frozen a piece of time, preserving itself in a perfect replica of the past. The ground all around became a dull white as the sun's light dimmed in the shadows, falling down the face of the mountain. Bits of green leaves peeked out from beneath fluffy layers of frost and snow that had drenched the trees and the land in color. Not a drop of snow fell though, and there was absolutely no trace of wind. There were no sounds in the air, only a hum coming from all around and from a great distance. It was a quiet hum, perhaps the sound of silence itself. My pace slowed greatly as I passed through such beauty. The colors were so unbelievably soothing and calming.

I moved onward and noticed over to my right, there was some sort of path or trail winding upward through the crevices. As I moved closer to the path, I was puzzled to see footprints leading down the mountain. In light of how hard I'd been working to reach the paradise I sensed was somewhere around the summit, it was hard to imagine why someone would leave such a wonderful place, and in such a hurry too. The stride was so far apart, and the marking so deep, this person had to have been running at a full clip.

For some reason I felt these markings were a good omen and that I was on the right track. I wondered how long ago the prints were made. It was only logical the prints would be covered up by the first strong snow but I had this overwhelming feeling nothing had changed in this area for eternities of time. If no snow had fallen, the prints could be as old as time itself.

The cold worked its way into my muscles and my body

wasn't responding so well to commands to move. I tripped and stumbled a few times because my legs didn't lift high enough to pass over a rock or step. The altitude also began to affect me greatly. My breathing was fast and heavy, and my body felt numb. A dull ache in my head and a light dizziness left my center of gravity askew. I sat down on a rock made of granite and tried to relax and catch my breath.

My sight faded into a fuzzy haze, and if I didn't pass out, I came right to the edge. My eyes weren't working correctly anymore, and things started to get dark. I looked up and saw shadows towering over me, looking down. I could have sworn I heard giggles. Maybe it was a ringing in my ear but I imagined they came from three beautiful women. The cold didn't bother them as they pranced around me in the snow with the most beautiful smiles. They all had the grace of fine ballerinas. As they danced around me, almost floating, I could feel them brushing against my skin and a rush of energy moved through my body. I felt what I must describe as love or at least some other word beginning with "L". I wanted to let go and immerse myself in their happiness and beauty. Maybe I'd found what I came for, beauty and love.

Inch by inch, they began to move down the path, all the while looking straight into my eyes, bouncing off the walls of my mind, and then flowing down into my heart. They were calling to me like the sirens. A sweet music was ringing in my ears. It was irresistible.

I wanted to believe so badly this was what I was searching for, but I knew this somehow was missing the mark, just another distraction or diversion designed with great care to reach into my depths and lure me into slavery. The calling went on. I tried to shut my ears and close my eyes but the sight was not coming from my eyes, and the noise was not coming from my ears. Both were in my mind. As I realized this, the beautiful images before me began to fade and the music tuned once again to the sounds of silence.

My heartbeat calmed and I was able to regain my wits. I was lying down on the snow-covered path as my breath returned. With great determination and stubbornness, I summoned my will and pressed up the path. My efforts were slow and labored, but I stumbled upward for hours more.

As I reached the cloud ceiling I looked up, and all around I saw a sea of white. What would I find above the clouds? I thought of the creatures that live just below the surface of the ocean and wondered if they realize an entire world exists just on the other side of the water. That's how I felt as I started into the cloud layer. I was about to discover a new world that had always existed yet I had never been aware of it.

A short while and the world below was lost in the haze of misty clouds. Above me and all around a haze emerged, nothing more than a misty white. I looked up, wondering what new world awaited. A doubt arose from deep caverns of thought. Was I fooling myself? What would I find on the other side? Maybe there is no God? Could this be nothing more than a chemical malfunction in my brain?

One doubt after another arose, and they all seemed to merge and take on an increased intensity. As they strengthened a crystallization took place until there before me my thoughts took form.

"My imprints are strongly on your soul."

Before me stood the most glorious and brilliant creature I'd ever imagined. I was in complete awe in its presence. Light was radiating outward in all directions. The shape indicated the being had taken on the form of a man. "This is all an illusion," he said, "You wanted to believe so badly, you created your own reality. The truth, however, is you have lost your mind. We've got to get you out of here! Hurry! Let's go! Follow me!"

"Where are we going?" I asked.

"Down off this mountain before you freeze to death! You're going to die up here!"

"I don't understand." I replied.

"You still don't understand? You've lost your mind! You're completely crazy! You've got to go back while you still can."

A bit of fear and uncertainty pulsed through my veins. The delight I'd experienced earlier was all but drained. I felt sick. I began to doubt the validity of the whole experience that had just taken place. I didn't realize where I was or what I was doing as the haze-like fog thickened. "What about Iron Ass and the secret society of light?"

"Fool! There is no Iron Ass! There is no secret society of light! You're nuts and you imagined this whole thing! Don't you understand yet? Haven't you figured it out?

"You're confused right now. Listen to me, trust me. Sweetheart, I'm trying to help you. I am you. These are your own thoughts trying to save your life. If you don't realize this, you're never going to be sane again. You're having hallucinations, and you're delirious. Please, listen to me. We need to get down off this mountain as quickly as possible. "

The man seemed to grow brighter as he continued to speak. "Child, I'm sorry things didn't work out for you in life. Life is tough. That's just the way it is. You can't escape from reality into some fantasy world where everything is ok, where everyone is kind. The truth is you want to hold on to fantasies and fairytales only children believe. You wanted to believe so badly that you actually convinced yourself of its truth.

"I'm sorry to be the one to tell you this, but it's because I love you. I don't want to see any more harm come to you. It's time to be like everyone else and deal with life as it is. You're having all these problems because you're messed up, Oliver. You're sad because there is something wrong with you. It's not the world that has the problem. The world doesn't need fixing. You do.

"I can tell you this because I am you. You are me. I'm the part of you that cares about you. Why else would I be up here trying to save your life? All the rest is lies. It's time to throw in the towel, Oliver. Be humble enough to admit you've failed in this ludicrous search for a heaven that never existed outside yourself in the first place.

"Trust me on this one. It's over, Oliver. Let's go down the mountain. Forget this spiritual poison from now on. Forget this fantasyland talk. Look what it's done to you. It's almost killed you, that's what it's done. Look what it's done to the world. People kill each other every day over the same delusions about fantasyland that you bought into.

"Admit it now or die trying but you need to let me take care of you for a while. Once you stop feeling sorry for yourself and admit you're messed up, *then* you can get better. Then you can take care of yourself. Then life won't be so hard for you.

"So you had a nervous breakdown. So your heart was broken. That's what happens to people in life. So what! Now let's get the hell out of here before you get so messed up you can never make it back and break the hearts of all your family and friends! If not for yourself, do it for them at least! Let's go!"

His words were so enticing, but what if this was the Grand Daddy of all Delusions? What if this was his greatest trick? Once and for all I had to make my decision. Who would I follow? That's when Iron Ass appeared.

"Why are you still listening to this crap!" he yelped, "It's the same old story all wrapped and packaged in new paper!"

"Are you telling me that was crap talking to me?" I said

"There is no way you will fit through the door with all the crap you're carrying on your back." Iron Ass snapped, "In fact, it would be a disservice if you were able. There is nothing you have to prove to God or anyone else. The truth is this is about accepting yourself and loving who you are. This is about realizing your true beauty and in so doing you will see that so much of what you have been taught is not true."

Iron Ass was finally starting to calm down. "Now is the time to search your heart for your truth. What you have been told and all the stories people tell are of no importance right now. Search your heart! The mind will never solve the puzzle. Choose your path, Oliver. Choose your path."

Standing before me stood Iron Ass. To my left stood the being of light who seemed so pure. I thought and thought but I couldn't see through the arguments.

"Is this all lies?" I screamed out.

"Well, somebody sure as hell is lyin' to ya an it's just the King of Crapola over here!" Iron Ass shouted, "Only your heart can hold the truth. Use your heart, Oliver. *Follow your heart*. There's no flaw in those words. Follow your heart."

A bare whisper was all I could manage, "God have mercy on my soul."

Divine timing must have been working magic as time shattered, returning me to the beach in spirit. It was the middle of the night, I was up to my neck in the ocean water as wave after wave crashed over me. I was reliving the moments of my first nights on the beach and I heard myself calling out, "My life is in the hands of Jesus Christ; my life is in the hands of Jesus Christ". As those words filled my ears, they were accompanied by an opening of my heart. The love of Christ came flowing. I didn't know the answer, I was experiencing it, I was living it, I was feeling it.

As tears rolled down my face, I screamed with all my heart, "I believe Jesus! I believe!"

"I choose life! I choose life! I choose life!"

Wrapped in the love and bliss of the Christ, I saw through the illusions my mind had created. The truth is, if people would take off the mask we wear just for a few moments, we would see that we are not alone. We are all the same. We all feel the same pains and the same joys. We isolate ourselves.

Iron Ass looked over with a smile on his face and a twinkle in his eye. For the first time, he spoke gently and calmly. He was filled with so much joy. "See, Oliver, it was already over from the beginning. The ending had already been written. You solved the puzzle long ago. Just learn to hold on to God's love. Never let it go."

I was still floating with the Divine when a loud scream shrieked out from nothingness. The scream was ever so smooth and carried a hollow, surreal quality, probably largely due to the way it seemed to be heard in the distance, echoing and then ringing out through the air. I will never forget that scream for all eternity.

"I'll never let him out!!!"

The creature telling me his lies had been exposed. Right before my eyes, in a transformation no less than Jekyll and Hyde, he turned into some kind of hideous monster - a demon of the mind, of course, but just as real as anything I've ever seen. The light coming off him had been no less than his greatest sleight-of-hand. He was a grotesque shadow sucking in light from every direction. He was the ultimate vampire of light and love, his sole purpose to rob the soul of its original state of grace. He had been soaking in so much of my own light, he had appeared to be glowing. With each additional word he spoke, I had been giving him more and more of my power until he shined like Lucifer himself. Once I saw through his delusions and lies, I reclaimed my own power, leaving him nothing more than a shadow devoid of life. His existence was being threatened when he screamed out, calling me back to his web.

I saw first-hand the creature was not really me. I gave it power, but it wasn't part of me. With its true face exposed, memories flashed through my vision. I saw this thing yelling and screaming constantly, analyzing this, speculating that, judging, plotting, scheming, and complaining. It told me how ugly and worthless I was. It was humbling and sad to see.

There was no way I was taking this with me to the other side. I was going to pull the plug on the power I had given him. It would return to the nothingness from which it emerged.

The scream was one of the last sounds I heard from the so-called friend. With that there came the quiet I haven't felt as long as I can remember. It's as if part of me has mysteriously fallen silent. Quiet stillness produces a calm that reaches deeply and completely into a tranquil pool.

The last clear words I heard came from Iron Ass. He had a warm smile on his face and his eyes told me how much he loved me and how proud he was.

"You have found your truth; now go live it. Find the door and remember; you've made your decision. On the other side what is left will be your garden, your truth. To pass through the dream world you must take this step."

The King of Crapola was having some kind of conniption fit but Iron Ass kept his relaxed demeanor and turned to me.

"What is released is no more."

King of Crapola turned to Iron Ass and he was yelling and screaming like a madman. He tried every tactic possible to get Iron Ass to listen to him, including crying like a baby. Nothing worked though. Iron Ass stood about three feet away, completely encased in a golden flame of light. He seemed to be totally at ease and at peace as he listened. "That's nice." I would hear him say as he nodded his head with a sly smirk spread across his face.

There's no doubt he was paying no attention to the King. I know because I've seen the same look on Doctor Ambika that Iron Ass was wearing. He listened to and then totally ignored or dimissed whatever I told him, as if I'd been too crazy to even put a sentence together! Oh well, but Iron Ass had the exact same smile on his face, combined with that little nod of his head. King of Crapola hates to be dismissed as an incoherent babbling liar. Iron Ass was putting on a fine demonstration in dealing with his lies.

With hope and faith I marched through the cloud layer. On the other side, I stood on a fluffy carpet of clouds gazing up at a wonderfully majestic palace. The gates were made of a shimmering gold, yet they would glimmer and reflect the blue and purple in the sky. Streaks of a green energy and light were leaking out through the palace walls and I realized the entire castle was made of light energy. In the middle of the golden gates I saw a door. Above the door, inscribed in deep green, were the words of Heraclitus. Maybe he wrote them, or maybe he remembered them and brought them to our world?

The Soul is dyed the color of its thoughts.
Think only on those things that are in line with your principles
and can bear the Full Light of Day. The content of your character
is your choice. Day by day, what you choose, what you think, and
what you do, is who you become. Your Integrity is your Destiny.
It is the Light that guides your way.

I took my time and let Heraclitus's words burn into my essence, and then I stepped through the door. Immediately I was surrounded and immersed in a foggy haze. I remembered the haze well as it started to wash over me. I was surrounded by nothingness. I seemed to be floating in a white fog that lulled me to sleep. The fog worked its magic upon me and the recent past began to lose its grip. What had been unquestionably real began to feel like a dream. I was being sucked into a new dream and I fought with all my strength to remain awake. It was no use though and the fog swirled in even tighter.

In my most lucid moments, I found myself in the inner room. The walls were quite high and the room was no more than ten by twelve. To the front of the room there was a wooden door with a small window. The whole place seems to be in white. A picture hangs in this heaven. A Divine Mother of sorts. It speaks of something so beautiful I cannot comprehend it. How can she remain so perfectly loving while some of her children are constantly in the presence of such great darkness? The secret is there. The secret is in her eyes. They know. She stares at the ending. It is so beautiful.

All my memories are softening, becoming less and less real. I've been writing as quickly as possible, I don't want a drop to be lost. Even the memory of Iron Ass now seems like just something I dreamt one night.

In the haze of fog I can see a white haired old man walking along a dirt-covered path. In his hand he has a large brush and he's carefully dusting away a set of footprints. I know the footprints are the path I walked while in the middle worlds. The old guy started sweeping the night of my dream. Like an Indian tracker, he's an expert at erasing my trail.

The fog keeps growing thicker and thicker, washing my mind of memories. The old man has followed the footprints and traced my steps right to the door of the castle.

"I beg you, spare the last memory."

With serenity, he touched his heart and placed a white rose and a single red rose in my hands. "These flowers are all that remain, you can take them with you," he said, "In time you will remember. Long ago, you heard a beautiful voice that constantly spoke to you. It sang you sweet songs and told you wonderful stories and fantasies. It would also tell you jokes, so you were always laughing and giggling with glee. One day, you stopped hearing that voice, and another replaced it. This voice was stern and unkind and constantly accused you, speaking of darkness and worthlessness. This voice was unforgiving and constantly told you lies. I promise you, once again the *loving voice* will be heard."

The fog only grows thicker now. My body is melting, dripping with anesthesia. The inner room is all that's left. My eyes are so heavy and tired. I'm so tired. I feel I'm going to sleep forever.

Twenty-Four

LOCK UP

The first time you find yourself insane and locked in a mental hospital is not only the lowest and saddest point in your life; it is also the most horrible, fear filled, and perfect reflection of Hell that exists on this earth. The second time isn't so bad, and the third? Let's keep our fingers crossed.

March 1st was *the last journal* entry. It's taken a long time for me to understand exactly what happened way back then. The rest of the story I can only give to you as my best recollection. Some parts are fuzzy while others are quite lucid. What matters is I have enough information to weave the thread that will tie the story together and provide all the pieces of the puzzle.

I couldn't remember writing the last journal entry or how I got where I was for that matter. My first memory was waking in a hospital. I say "waking" because that's the best way to put it. I could have been sitting there all day long, but I have no memory whatsoever of what I had been doing before that. It was like a light switch being flipped on, and there I was, looking at my cell. It was as if I had been born in that instant with no memories from the past, no worries, no fears, no thoughts. If I'd turned around to look into the past, the path would seem to have emerged about five or ten minutes earlier from a light mist that eventually turned into a dense, black fog. The fog was the hazy dream I'd been living in the weeks before. Iron Ass, the beach, the sunset – they had all been the substance and product of delusion. As Iron Ass said "All here is an illusion". He fully understood what really happened. I hadn't been living at the beach at all. I was in a psychiatric ward. It took all my heart and strength to accept where I was.

In the end, it was powerful doses of anti-psychotic medication that sucked me back into another dream, the one we are living now. We call it reality, but for me, everything has since looked rather suspect. Perhaps one day I will unlock the door to an even greater truth. Are we possibly living a dream? The mystics often say just this. Not real, but not unreal either. Could life be the most incredible experience of them all, the ultimate virtual reality - a journey through a world that is actually comprised of nothing more than shadow and light, designed and held together so tightly by our limited senses that we cannot see the forces that are the underlying existence and final truth? Even now, science is discovering secrets of the universe that seem to confirm what the ancient sages have said all along: everything is comprised of energy. Nothing is truly solid. Our reality is sculpted by our thoughts, opinions, and beliefs derived from the instruments that we have been given to explore and interact with life, our five senses. This is the human experience, but what lies beyond? I have been on a journey to discover the answer for a while now, beginning with the first pieces of the puzzle I received during my breakdown in what I call the middle worlds.

The day I realized where I really was, was breathtaking. My first experience was simply being aware I was conscious, that I was alive. The experience flowed effortlessly and smoothly into my first emotion, a deep and penetrating peace that wrapped around me in a bubble of fresh air. I could barely think. I could barely move. Drugged to a near comatose state, I was so doped up on medication I probably couldn't have said my name. Then I looked up and saw her. She was an angel if I've ever seen one - my mom. She was sitting with a smile, quietly reading. In her lap rested my journal. She must have realized I noticed her.

"This is quite a story you have here, Oliver," she said sweet-ly, "I'm so glad I decided to read what you've been writing all these days. We would have never known you were pretending to take your medication."

I tried to speak but I couldn't manage to harness enough brainpower to make a sound.

"They had to blast you with a ton of medication to get you back," she said.

And then my mom began to tell me about the last month of my life, starting with the day my eyes were opened to the love within in a sudden rip of a veil separating two worlds - January 24, 1992. I know those around me remember that day well, but the story they tell is much different than my own.

My mom got the call around 10:00 p.m. On January 24th, as I rode with my fraternity to our yearly party, the doors to the netherworld were creaking open. By the time the party was in full swing, I was falling into the shadowy caverns of my mind. In the middle of my crazed state at the bar, the flood-gates of my heart were released. I found myself running around in a panic, and it was that panic that led me in search of one quarter so I could call my mom and tell her how much I loved her before I died.

Mom was getting ready for bed when the call came. For an instant, she had no idea who was on the other end of the line but she sensed something desperate was happening. I kept telling her over and over how much I loved her with all my heart. She immediately assumed I was intoxicated or some-thing terrible had happened to me. Her first instinct was panic. She knew her son very well and couldn't comprehend why he would be in such a state.

"What's wrong? Are you all right? Where are you?"

I proceeded to tell her all that had happened that night. I was totally crazed and no one around seemed to be paying any attention to me. Over and over she kept asking where I was but I just kept repeating the same thing: "You'll find me in your heart."

Right after that, some kind of fear came over me and I hung up the phone. My mom was frantic and had no idea what to do. She began calling everyone she knew who might know me or possibly tell her where I was. Tears were running down her cheeks from her sweet blue eyes as she called one person after another. Finally she was able to get a close friend of mine who was willing to help. He is the only fraternity brother I've kept in touch with all these years. I actually met a handful of genuinely good people in the house, fun characters - mostly pledge bothers, but I lost touch, choosing to live a different life. The friend who my mom finally got ahold of that night is also spiritually inclined so perhaps that's why we stayed connected. We both love fishing, the ocean, surfing, mountains, and nature. He's very creative, deeply intuitive, and like me, sensitive. The difference between us is that he is still trying to live life as intensely as possible. He is trying to get every last ounce of emotion from the adventure he is on. This makes him a very interesting and alluring fellow to the great majority of people who meet him. I am always impressed with his insights and ability to stay focused while maintaining balance all while indulging in the great pleasures of life that are so often peddled to us as honey-coated treats. For many they turn to sharpened razors, but over the years I've watched him endure and stay afloat while many around him drop off the edge in addiction or other traps. To me, what matters is that he finds true happiness. So far, his self-discipline has enabled him to live the divine comedy of life in a way that most would never dare. Most certainly, by the end of his days, he will have some incredible stories to tell, and he will have learned a great deal about the drama of life. No one can say that he hasn't embraced his existence with passion. I think this is his fuel and it has made him a fantastic artist.

When my mom finally got him on the phone, the search parties went out. While I was in the midst of a complete break from reality, my mom, my sister, my dad, and my friend were all out searching for me. I can only imagine the pain that my parents were feeling as they tried to locate me. My friend assumed I was on drugs and told this to my mom. This only heightened her fear that I was going to somehow kill myself. She was beyond panic, not even able to cry or take a second to think of herself.

While it's true, during my semester as a pledge I tried some drugs for the first time in my life, I was not intoxicated in any way when I had my first experience with bipolar mania nor had someone slipped me some acid. One of the first things the doctors did was to test me for the entire spectrum of drugs. There were none. In hindsight, it began with a mild break during my initiation. During my time with the fraternity, my drug resume consisted of: marijuana ten to fifteen times, "ecstasy" four or five times, and "magic mushrooms" once. I am certainly no angel. The big question to me, and probably held quietly in the hearts of my family, is whether trying these drugs changed the chemistry of my mind and prepped me for my eventual breakdown? Like the effects of my fraternity initiation, we will never know the answer. Some doctors say I would have eventually been overcome by the illness nonetheless, and others say it's possible that I might have escaped it. I do know this; however, I would not be who I am today without having gone through the tremendous suffering, the turmoil, and the rapture that I experienced.

After an intense and desperate search, my mom and friend

were able to locate me, or at least where I had been, and where I was taken. They were a bit too late at the bar. After the call to my mom, I collapsed. When people saw what had happened the party came to a halt. The music stopped, strobe lights shut down, and the main lights came on. The only noise came from the panic and worry in the air.

There I was, lying all sprawled out on the floor, totally crazed. The paramedics arrived and luckily understood I was in some form of psychosis. They took my body to the hospital, but I have a feeling my mind was already tucked in my bed and staring at the sheet above me in my home at school.

If I try my best to focus, I can remember that day. I do remember the ambulance picking me up. I even remember arriving at the mental hospital. Why my mind refused to acknowledge this, I still don't know. I found myself in a room with a steel bed in the middle. The walls were about fifteen feet high and the room was no more than ten by twelve. To the front of the room there was a solid door with a tiny square window right in the middle. I wandered over and looked through the window. There was another larger room on the outside with white ceramic tile floor. In fact, the whole place seemed to be in white. The door wouldn't open so I wandered around the room. I wasn't sure if it was night or day. High in the corner of the room there was a tiny window that light was coming through but I couldn't see sky. I thought maybe the light was there to trick me into thinking it was daytime. I was sure someone was holding me captive and they were trying to brainwash me. I was a prisoner.

As it turns out, I was in Charter Hospital. I was being held on a 72-hour hold. A doctor or nurse came in and explained where I was and what was going to happen. Of course I didn't believe a word he said. To begin with, he kept telling me I was a danger to myself and a danger to others. That just didn't make sense. I knew I wasn't a danger to myself and I'd never

ever hurt anyone else yet he kept telling me I was. And that was the key. He was *telling* me I was a danger to others. "You are a danger to others," he kept saying.

Well, since I knew I was being held in prison and people were trying to brainwash me, telling me that I'm supposed to be dangerous to others obviously meant some sick cult had me as a prisoner, and they were trying to program me. Once I realized that, I really wised up and I started to play along with the little game.

They wanted to give me medication and there was no way in hell I was going to let them poison me. "You take it first!" I said. Their refusal only confirmed my thoughts, so I laughed at them for thinking I was stupid enough to let them give me some mind controlling drugs. "You're telling me you want me to take this but you won't even take it yourself? No way am I taking anything."

The first guy that came in must have spent a couple of hours with me and I have no idea what crazy things I told him. He left and brought me some food to eat. There was no way I was going to fall for his little trick. I was way too smart to eat the food they poisoned.

Fortunately, my memory was shot too and after an hour of being alone I looked over, saw a plate of food, and I devoured the whole thing in a few minutes. At that point a nurse came in. She was very kind and had such a gentle voice. She told me she had to take a sample of my blood. I was sure she was poisoning me but I sat quietly while my blood poured out of my arm into the syringe. It felt as if she was shooting something into me and to this day I don't know if it was medication or she actually was taking my blood.

Either way, I became really tired and I tried to sleep. The bed was hard and cold and the room I was in was freezing. There were all kinds of sounds and loud noises. I became more and more convinced that these people were trying to brainwash me. They were trying to confuse me until I didn't know up from down and then they would tell me whatever they wanted. The noises and the cold were all tricks to break me. These people were trying to suck me into their world by making me think that I was crazy.

I sat there in that cell, just waiting. I was waiting for the walls around me to vanish and to wake up in some paradise. I would close my eyes and try to will myself into that other world where I wanted to go. Each time, when I opened my eyes, I was still in the cold, ugly cell.

The nurse came back, and she brought me some more food, which I ate without a thought. It didn't matter if they were poisoning me anyway. I wanted to die. I wished for death with all my heart. The food made me even sleepier and I fell asleep.

When I woke up I found the door to my cage open and I wandered out into the hall. There was a big, carpeted room with a TV and magazines and a nice soft couch. The lights were dim. It must have been the middle of the night. Two big and strong doors locked in the whole unit. A sign hung above that said "Elopement Risk". When I read the sign, I got a bit excited because I thought I might be getting married.

There was no one else up - everyone must have been asleep - and I wandered around for a bit. Every once in a while I would hear the intercom come on. "Paging Doctor Ambika. . paging Doctor Ambika".

Sometime during the night, a woman came walking down the hall. She had blonde hair and trusting blue eyes. Now I know that was my mom. The minute I saw her something hit me right in the heart. I knew her but I just couldn't place where. She sat down with me and started a nice conversation. Or at least I think it was. Who knows what I really said? I told her my story as best as I could.

The beautiful blonde angel took out a quarter and gave it to me. "Here," she said, "this quarter is for hope. Everything will be alright."

I took the quarter and went back to my cell where I tried to fall asleep. The room was too uncomfortable, and I couldn't though. I refused to realize I was in a hospital. The deeper part of me was already sitting on the beach at Ollie's Peak waiting for the sunset. My heart was breaking more and more every second and I took out my quarter. I held onto it as tightly as I could, right up against my chest where my heart was. The pain was unbearable, and I took my quarter and I threw it across the room.

I sat there without hope for a few minutes and then I went over and picked it up. I held on to it as tightly as I could and then I cursed God and I threw it across the room. A few minutes later I picked it up again and repeated the same process. Over and over I went through this ritual and maybe somehow through it I learned that I can never give up hope for too long. It always comes back to me. I think that's one of the lessons I learned during my time in the middle worlds.

It was on Wednesday, March 4th, 1992 at 6:12 a.m. when I snapped out of it. For over a month, while my mind was roaming the beaches of my youth, my body had been locked up. All I could think was some miracle had happened because once again I felt so clean and new.

I wasn't kept in the hospital much longer but during that time I had visits from just about all my friends. My parents came by for dinner every day and my sister would visit whenever she could. They were there for me the whole time and I can't imagine the strength a person must have to make it through such an earthshaking experience without the support of family. People I'd totally forgotten about came by and it wound up being like one big welcome-back party. Everyone who came by seemed so full of life.

Of course my doctor, Doctor Ambika, was there every day

as well. While I choose to put my life in the hands of God, I have to share that I have had a tremendous amount of help from doctors and modern medicine. I have been very careful not to reveal my history with medication for fear that I may influence someone in any way. The fact is that this is a very personal condition, which takes on many forms, and has a wide spectrum of effects. Medication is one of the tools available. Some are in a place where they need it, and others may get by without it. Ultimately, it can be a life or death decision.

After I felt better and my mind was stronger, I went home to my parent's house, but there was one more thing I had to do. For some reason, I had to return to my place at school and watch the sunrise. I felt the urge from the minute I woke up in the hospital. I think maybe it was some way of symbolizing closure and a new start to life. For some reason I felt so fresh and excited. There seemed so many opportunities and so many things to do. I couldn't quite place where these feelings were coming from, but I felt I'd been given a new start in life. Something had happened that changed the world. I could see it all around me. It was almost hard to believe. The nurses were so friendly, and everyone I came across seemed interesting and funny in their own way. The feeling reminds me a bit of the way I felt when I was young. Everything seemed shiny and exciting. Sometimes I could barely contain my joy and I'd find myself laughing out-loud for no reason. The doctors said it was just the medication they were giving me, but I wonder. I wished so much to know or understand why the entire world looked different to me.

What's funny is I think my mom helped me to capture the right words. Knowing what I do now, they seem hauntingly prophetic.

"We thought it looked like you weren't coming back," she said to me.

"I *changed* my mind."

Twenty-Five

THE SUNRISE

*A*round 4:00 a.m. I returned to my place at school. I still see it so clearly I can return to the moment almost anytime and remember every detail. I remember hearing the deck outside my window creak as my first steps hit the ground in my room. I remember walking into the dimly lit room and scanning it from left to right. Everything seemed so utterly real. Above my bed, hanging from the ceiling, was my crazy sheet with all its colors and designs. The room was as if no one had touched it. It seemed so long ago I lived there, but there were no cobwebs. The bed was made all tidy and the rest of the room looked nice and clean, yet it held deep emotions.

I couldn't wait for the morning sunlight to inch its way over the top of the mountains. Soon light would be filling the sky and seeping in through the windows. A thought washed over me. I opened the side door, walked out onto the decking, and sat down. We always kept a chair on the deck for relaxing. I walked over and sat down. I had waited so long to see the sunrise.

Even though I couldn't remember much of it, the experience had taken its toll on body and mind. I simply couldn't fight my emotions. I just wanted to sit down and watch the sunrise in peace. I wrapped myself up in a huge fleece blanket. I had on my nicest pair of sweatpants. The blanket was all white and gray and the sweatpants were charcoal black.

I sat before the dawn waiting. The sun steadily and confidently began to make its way over the top of the mountains. Its first rays of light came floating down through the sky. At this moment, I felt the first tear dribble down my cheek. It was a tear of joy and with it came the first piece of my puzzle, the first drop of my story. As the tear rolled off my chin, I heard a beautiful and gentle voice bubble up from deep within. The voice was familiar, because it was my own. The message was so very sweet.

"Do you want to write this down?"

The answer didn't have time to register in my brain. So much love was pouring out of me I couldn't stand to lose even a drop. Instantly, almost simultaneously, I was up out of my seat and looking for some paper and a pen inside the house.

I returned to the patio and without hesitation, I began to write. The words flowed so smoothly. They started in my heart as an emotion, moving to my mind where they became words, and finally through my finger-tips right onto the page in front of me.

I've awakened this morning with a peace I haven't felt in so very long. Always I've felt that during the night I journey to the most beautiful places soaked in love and I return drenched in their graces. I'm looking out over my patio and I see the mountains and rolling hills covered by the tops of green trees as they stretch across the valley. It's amazing what can grow in the desert when a bit of water is added. Having to run the sprinklers every day is most certainly a small price to pay for this beauty that I have seen every day and only this morning do I finally return its efforts by telling nature how beautiful she is and that I will never take her for granted. In truth, I never have, I simply haven't encountered words beautiful enough to thank her with.

So this morning my suspicions are finally confirmed, for some reason I am permitted to float through the realms of heaven, and in the morning, even though my conscious has trouble remembering, my soul is again filled with the waters of love. Part of these blessings might be spent sitting with a poet I've known since the beginning of time. She recites her beauty and when I leave her I must say such a powerful prayer . . . that I might remember just one or two sentences of what flowed from her lips! Perhaps this journal and even a wonderful story were written ages ago and now all I have is to remember their words?

I feel each day I move closer to my heart, the more I will remember on the soul level. How wonderful it will be on the day when mind, heart, and soul are one! On that day there will be no forgetting or time lag in the messages of my beautiful poetess.

The early morning air is crisp but not biting and as I look up over the mountains I see a crystal clear sky, deep blue in the heavens and fading to the lightest of blues as it finally mixes with the gentle whites of the mist and fog.

For so long, I've thought there were no fruits from my journey, and as I now look out above the fog and above the mist, I can imagine a city. Its gates are gold and palaces rise up higher and higher into the heavens. The colors are indescribable, with radiance I cannot comprehend, and this is only the outermost edge of this wonderful place!

The architecture is not of this world, all is flowing and smooth yet defined and with individual personality. Perhaps only gentle and constant waters could create such a shape? And now I see that I have not been wasting time or been lazy

. . . *You see the builder of this city is myself. I have ham-mered in every last nail. I can almost feel the smile of the wisdom that has built this paradise because today I have dis-covered the secret ahead of its time. How cunning and wise is the creator that even while I paved the streets and put in the stain glass windows, I did not realize I was building some-thing, anything! My eyes must have been closed. What a gift, to be able to explore all of heaven simply by entering through the door within my heart.*

Oliver, I am writing this journal to let you in on a few se-crets and maybe lead you to a small window. If you ever might want to perch your arms on the sill and look inside you'll know where to look.

There are mysteries in life that many of us ignore or simply refuse to believe. Our five senses define for us what our reality is to be. We become prisoners of these senses in that any things that do not fall into their spectrum are considered unre-al. Some day we will all learn that this is simply not so. What about the wonderful and inspiring stories of guardian angels? Or the amazing stories of those who return from a near death experience with glorious tales of another world, an-other side of life that is filled with fairies and beings of light? What about moments when we are filled with an intuition so strong and powerful we cannot ignore the sensations, intuition that saves lives and prevents tragedies. What about brief mo-ments of grace when one senses a presence only to be suddenly brushed by God in an instant of peace and perfection?

In the jungle of our backyard, the birds are singing, but all remains somehow still and quiet. I'm taking a deep breath and feeling a tired relief wash over my entire body. First my neck loosens and then peace trickles down my throat and out into my arms and fingertips. The breath then flows even deep-er into my lungs and down into my stomach, washing inside my legs where it all comes to rest at my feet. This thing is fi-

nally over and I've learned an incredible lesson. I feel there is more to what went on than I know, lessons just waiting to bubble into my awareness at their proper time. Whatever these teachings are, I feel they are already within and maybe I just have to remember them?

The flood of thoughts, emotion, and wisdom that washed through my head makes me feel the inside of my brain has taken some form of mind bath. All the rust and grime were stirred up and finally blown from my mind in a flood that almost killed me. Was this just the price I had to pay? Why am I so filled with a burning desire to remember the thoughts and ideas that passed through my mind in those instants? Could there be method to madness? Maybe somehow I was able in brief moments to connect with my deeper self? Messages and information were given to me that seem to be trying to tell me something or give me some kind of wisdom. Maybe during the turmoil my conscious mind was enduring, a part of me that I normally couldn't hear got its chance and was able to speak to me? Maybe this was the only time I was listening? The voice still seems to ring within the walls of my head. It was calm and sweet and seemed to emanate from within.

I wonder where that loving voice came from. It emerged from the chaos like a beautiful flower spreading its warm and brilliant colors into my world. It gave me a sense of peace, something to hang onto during the horrors and hallucinations that were all around. The loving and soothing voice actually became my Shepherd during the night.

It wasn't just the voice or what it said that gave me comfort, more so it was the way it made me feel; serene, calm, tranquil. It seems such a paradox and is near impossible to capture on paper, how there can be something so beautiful present when all around there is darkness. Perhaps the best I can do is to say that in the midst of chaos and turmoil there was a loving presence watching over me. Not just watching over me but actually speaking to me, comforting me, guiding me. Sometimes this loving force spoke with soothing words, and other times she would take on the form of an inspiring song or even the faint outline of a rainbow in the sky. Whatever way she revealed herself, the feeling was always the same, it was love itself, expressed in soothing feelings and emotions. I hope I don't forget those moments. You see, at first there was just fear and only when things got too intense I would feel her presence. Most of the time I felt alone and my fears did what they wanted with me.

Gradually, each time I felt her love, I began to recognize her presence, her scent. As if I were learning to write poetry, I became clearer and better at detecting her songs. At first it took a bit of imagination to hear the words and to realize the forms she expressed herself to me as. Colors, music, kind words, moments of joy, emotions, they were all ways in which she spoke. Slowly, but oh so deliberately, I began searching for this feeling of tranquility to comfort me during the panic and fear. The more I sought out this feeling, the more I felt it. The more I felt it, the easier it was to find, and the deeper I felt it.

At first, the path to this feeling was covered with weeds and trees and rocks and thorns, but with each trip, a road began to form. After time the trip along the path began to pave itself until the road was filled with beauty from beginning to end. The path became more and more peaceful, and whenever I felt fear, anxiety, or any emotion that was unpleasant, I would walk along this path and soon I would feel her presence. In her light, everything was safe and nothing could ever hurt me. Whatever trouble was causing me fear, it was only an illusion and the fear faded.

During the darkness, listening for this music became my sole purpose. It was all I lived for and it was what kept me going. I'm writing about this music because I don't want this

180

treasure to be lost in the fog. I don't want to forget the feeling.
I don't want to forget the music.

Oliver, the reason I say this and the reason I'm writing
this for you is because in the midst of this horrible night of suffering, you truly have been given a great treasure. The treasure
is the music and once again you know how to listen for it. If
you forget the feeling, the road you paved will fade and you will
forget how to hear the songs of creation. This is a gift of magic
because the truth is, the songs and miracles are not played at
certain and specific moments in time, the truth is they are constantly being sung. So travel this path regularly and it will
grow more and more brilliant with each trip. And stop traveling on those other paths that bring hurt and sorrow to your
life. Some of these have been traveled so much they are like
highways, but rest assured, the less you use them the more they
will fade. How you behave in the present moment holds the
key. Eventually old paths will dry up, and plants and trees
will replace the roads until you no longer have the desire to
travel to places of sorrow.

Travel the roads of beauty, they will grow stronger and you
can create your own world of beauty, but remember, with this
gift you can also create the roads of darkness and misery.
Whatever thoughts and actions you choose to reinforce the
stronger that road will be. So simply remember the roads that
are paved by love and joy and the music of God. Remember
how they sound. Remember, there is love all around us. Feel
it! As hard as it may be, let the other roads fade and by using
the tools of conscious thought and action, you can become whoever you wish to be. Think of your mind as a garden and
plant beautiful flowers, flowers that make you feel wonderful
and alive. Take care of this garden, what you put in, and
how you nurture it. Whatever you put in your mind becomes
a part of you. Let the lures and troubles of the world fade,
and fill your mind with the qualities you cherish most: love,

peace, joy, and freedom. Don't give power to other thoughts. If your heart is filled with love, then you can feel love in everything. This is a key to heaven.

Oliver, you have been given a great gift. It is the key to a magic that is unquenchable. It might not make life a fairy tale, but it can enliven every moment, lacing life with wonder and amazement. And even when pain and sorrow might cross your path, just remember in the midst of all the uncertainty, there truly is love walking with you, holding your hand, singing to you, guiding you, protecting you, and unconditionally loving you. This is a love that contains all the fairy tales in all of creation. It is filled with beings who watch over us and love stories that will never end. This love and its angels are all too real, as real as the sun and moon, and their songs tell us the same things. Live life to the fullest, love to the fullest, and remember the beauty of life. This magic puts the highs in perspective, brighter and more lucid. It makes the lows more bearable. It assures us "All is well". The key is the music. Remember it! Listen for it! Time will fade, and so will its memories but the lessons of love and its music will remain.

When I finally stopped writing, the sun was high above. Emotion after emotion had swept over me with each word I captured and wrote down. I felt the entire spectrum of my life. I was left with the calm feeling of tranquility. For the first time, I was fully alive, yet utterly grounded. I saw reality as it was, accepted it, surrendered to it, and embraced it. I found the magic hidden within the ordinary as I sat for a few more moments and simply enjoyed the morning air. Nothing seemed to bother me and as I basked in this glow some last words bubbled to the surface. With these words came an image. I saw a beautiful red rose in full bloom accompanied by a white rose beginning to open its petals. It seems to me I could have saved myself many, many hours of suffering if I'd just written this last message first.

"Fill your life with love & joy, follow your heart, try your best, and love those around you. You can never go wrong on this path. Love expands. This is learning through love, and it is all God asks of us. . . a complicated thing . . . what seems complicated . . . made easy."

The   End   .   .   . Thank God!!!

After-Word

THE STORYTELLER SPEAKS

Sometimes, when all the magic and forces in the universe are just right, someone escapes and rises above the dream. The chain and shackles rust, snap, or simply fade away. An ending? Definitely not! A new beginning!

The beauty of this story is the ending was already written long ago. In fact, if you caught it, it was the very first thing I wrote. This way, the most beautiful of love stories can be lived without any fear of failure. No matter how hard we try to fight the current, the characters always end up downstream in a quiet pool where peace and joy live. This is where the old is turned into the new and endings become beginnings, a place where travelers gather after their long journeys.

I've been working on this painting, *For Those Who Awaken*, for quite a while, well over ten years to date. A few months after my twentieth birthday, a week or two after my fraternity's ritual, I had the dream included in this book. The message was clear . . . "You are going to fight a great battle". Whatever fabric that weaves the fibers of reality together unraveled. I became lost, not knowing where I was, what was taking place, or even whether I was alive or dead. Then the hallucinations started. I feel my faith protected me.

The end result was a trip to Charter Hospital. There I battled the forces of psychosis, for pretty near forty days. It was one hell of a storm. With the help of doctors, my family, friends, I was able to gain a foothold. The battle I fight has now become more of a balancing act. I can honestly say God has given me all the tools I need to keep my sails flying true.

The doctors call my struggle bipolar illness. In truth, I've haven't really entertained the idea that I have an illness until now. The creativity, insights, and connection to some kind of beauty have always seemed like a gift - a gift with a price. At what point or what level of suffering does something turn from a gift into an illness? I think this depends on the experience. What intensity level is too much? When does it become abnormal? As I've studied healing and spirituality, I've come across people who sit on both sides of the river. I tend to be in the middle. I've been to both sides and I understand that suffering can be very real and tough to get over, to let go of the memory. I've also experienced truly wonderful and enchanting moments over the last ten years but I've been so very fortunate, blessed if you can call it that. I immediately found a path to walk. I had great friends, and a loving family. I poured all my energy into the spiritual pursuit and found positive ways to frame my experience. After my awakening, I found my interest in this world bleeding away only to be replaced by a profound desire for spiritual knowledge. I studied every text that fell into my grip. Often, in the silence of the night, I would be reading from the bible given to me when I was a child. I found great insight in the mastery of the mind demonstrated by the Buddha and the yogis of Tibet and India. Their stories assured me that my efforts to learn how to balance my mind and body would not be wasted. I saw the evidence chiseled before me in their lives. The wisdom traditions and words of mystics provided clear and precise validations of my own experiences. I have been shown the light that underlies what I've been through. I see the good times as well as the bad. What I've tried to share, is that illness or blessing, there is a gift and silver lining that can be found within the experiences of our lives, the highs and lows, whether one is diagnosed by a doctor or simply feeling the full spectrum of life.

In *For Those Who Awaken*, I wanted to create a painting that starts as nothing and slowly takes form until the last few strokes of my brush reveal a picture that is really quite beautiful. As I wrote earlier, this was my best attempt to capture my experience on canvas. In my painting, darkness had to be used. It makes all the other colors seem more intense and vibrant. It gave them life. It brought out their true beauty. The painting is abstract and surreal, inspired by my own experience, memories, imagination, and creativity. Every color has a root in the dark nights of my soul. Once again, I deeply feel I have framed a portrait that reflects the experience of my heart and it is my heart I have shared with you.

Flowing from the dawn came a time of great wonder, of great sorrow, and great healing. I can see the magical threads of experience carefully wound together in perfect balance and perfect harmony, just as they were meant to be. Much like the effortless flow of a winding river, it is destiny that has made me who I am. And who I am constantly emerges from that dark night of my soul ten years ago, blazing like a sacred flame within, hollowing out my very being so an even greater self could emerge.

As I watch the ease with which the waters flow, resisting nothing, I can only smile and wonder at my own struggle with life since the day of my awakening. Yet here I am, filled with peace, saturated with hope, smiling knowing that something pure and beautiful exists in all of us, in all living things, in all things.

I have chosen to seek healing in the sanctuary of my own spirit and my connection to the Great Spirit. Much of my time has been spent studying yoga and meditation. I've found beauty in many places. There have also been struggles with depression rising and falling in my life. Like the ripening of grapes, somehow, I think the struggle has made me a better person.

The river continues its course, and the waters rise and fall, just as the moon waxes and wanes. Often I sit by the water's edge, let go of the old and become the new. Maybe for a moment I, too, am flowing as water, and here all is still, all is peace, all is sacred, and all sorrows are washed away. In an instant, lightning may flash across the sky, and in a moment, awakening dawns. This is not just my story, my frozen moment out of time, when the sky was illuminated and a tiny spark of spirit was born amidst the terror of great darkness. From that light, new beings and new lives emerge.

... *A*nd so the knocking on The Door continues. The Princess never ceases to sing her songs. The melodies resonate from the magical book resting on her lap. It is always the tale of a great journey. Just on the other side, yet a world away, a faint whisper may be heard in the stillness. The Siren reaches to the night, calling her children home.

Much Love and Blessings,

Ollie

Made in the USA
San Bernardino, CA
15 April 2014